T0329274

CAMBRIDGE LIBRARY COLLECTION

Books of enduring scholarly value

Cambridge

The city of Cambridge received its royal charter in 1201, having already been home to Britons, Romans and Anglo-Saxons for many centuries. Cambridge University was founded soon afterwards and celebrates its octocentenary in 2009. This series explores the history and influence of Cambridge as a centre of science, learning, and discovery, its contributions to national and global politics and culture, and its inevitable controversies and scandals.

Wordsworth at Cambridge

In 1950 St John's College marked the centenary of William Wordsworth's death with a day of talks and celebrations, focusing on the poet's connections with the college and the University. This volume of material taken from the college magazine The Eagle describes college life in the poet's time and reproduces speeches and toasts given on the commemoration day by the Master, Fellows and guests. It also includes a record by the famous bibliographer A.N.L. Munby of the items with Wordsworth connections owned by St John's: an inscribed copy of his Poetical Works, which he gave to the College in 1832, a number of other first editions, and of course his signature in the college register. The book concludes with a descriptive catalogue of 34 known portraits of Wordsworth taken from life, some of which are reproduced in this volume.

Wordsworth at Cambridge

A Record of the Commemoration Held at St John's College, Cambridge in April 1950

ST JOHN'S COLLEGE

CAMBRIDGE
UNIVERSITY PRESS

CAMBRIDGE UNIVERSITY PRESS

Cambridge New York Melbourne Madrid Cape Town Singapore São Paolo Delhi

Published in the United States of America by Cambridge University Press, New York

www.cambridge.org
Information on this title: www.cambridge.org/9781108002899

This edition first published 1950
This digitally printed version 2009

ISBN 978-1-108-00289-9

CONTENTS

ILLUSTRATIONS

PORTRAIT OF WORDSWORTH IN RED AND BLACK CHALK
BY H. W. PICKERSGILL
IN SENIOR COMBINATION ROOM
No. 15

THE
WORDSWORTH
CENTENARY

THERE was bound to be something paradoxical about a celebration of the centenary of the death of Wordsworth in a university; however much pleasure and profit he may have derived from his career at St John's—and we have his own testimony that he did in fact derive from it much of both—no one could claim that his was an academic spirit, even in the widest sense of that word, or that for him the world of Cambridge was endowed with anything like the vitality or significance of the mountains of Switzerland or the Lakes. We were celebrating a man who is almost unanimously regarded as the greatest of Johnians, but whose latent genius was never apparent during the course of his university career. So the College, in celebrating the occasion, made no attempt to steal the thunder of those who were appropriately gathered at Grasmere and elsewhere in Lakeland to honour him in his own home, and did not set out to make the occasion anything more than a purely domestic one. Attention was concentrated on Wordsworth's Cambridge career, and it was frankly recognized that the greatest of his work and the most significant part of his career lay outside our scope.

The Master and Fellows of the College were present with their wives, and they had invited several distinguished members of other colleges as well as some old Johnians and some present scholars and research students of the College. The company assembled at midday on Saturday, 22 April, in the Combination Room, and had first the pleasure of hearing the Master.

ADDRESS BY THE MASTER
St John's College in Wordsworth's time

IT was the 30th October 1787 when, with his uncle, William Cookson, and his cousin, John Myers, Wordsworth arrived in Cambridge. Crossing the old Bridge, they alighted at the Hoop Hotel, where King and Harper's garage now stands. Cambridge was at the time a small country town, not yet 10,000 in population. The streets were unpaved and unlighted and gutters ran down the middle of them. The University numbered about 800 and the relations between Town and Gown were extremely hostile.

Wordsworth chose St John's because his uncle was at the time a Fellow of the College and a friend of one of the tutors. The Reverend William Cookson had been Preceptor to three of the King's sons and was a man of some influence. He wished to help the young Wordsworths who were orphans and in financial difficulty. William, he trusted, would win a fellowship at College and take orders and thus be provided for.

Through most of the eighteenth century St John's had been the largest College in the University, but Trinity was now gaining the lead in numbers and academical honours. St John's had the character of the Tory College in the Whig University. Its reputation had been much increased by the vigorous policy of Dr William Powell, Master from 1765 to 1775, who had raised the educational standard and given much attention to the grounds and buildings. The government of the College was still regulated by the Statutes of Queen Elizabeth, and the men who tried to make the College efficient under these obsolete rules deserve a credit that they seldom get.

The thing was being done of course in the truly English way of introducing the new under the forms of the old. The statutory College lectureships, like most of the University professorships, had become sinecures and the life of the College had passed into the tutorial system. The tutors took charge of the education of the under-graduates. Originally all the Fellows had had pupils who shared their rooms and whom they taught. By Wordsworth's time the number of tutors had come down to two or three, each of whom employed other Fellows as assistant tutors or lecturers.

Wordsworth's tutor, Edward Frewen, was the son of a well-known physician. He was an experienced College officer, and at the age of forty-one had just become one of the seniority—the eight senior Fellows, who, with the Master, administered the affairs of the College. So far as formal duties went, he certainly looked after his pupils' interests. Wordsworth had been admitted as a sizar—the usual thing for an able boy of limited means, and, within a week of coming into residence, he was elected a Foundress' Scholar. His Tutor procured for him also two small exhibitions, which helped to eke out a slender income, and assigned him inexpensive rooms.

These rooms were the lowest middle chamber over the kitchen, looking into the Back Lane, in which a bedroom had been partitioned off to form a somewhat dark cupboard, with a little window into the keeping room. At this time rooms were numbered consecutively through the three courts. The last set was numbered 103 and Wordsworth's was number 23, reached from staircase F in the First Court, then called Pump staircase. Fellows and Fellow Commoners were for the most part in the First and Second Courts and other members of the College in the Third Court and the Labyrinth—the old monastic building behind the Chapel.

In 1876 Wordsworth's rooms were made into a storeroom and later on were thrown into the kitchen to give more air space. Stained glass in the window bears the inscription

> William Wordsworth 1787–1791
> My abiding place, a nook obscure.

In the spring of 1839 Wordsworth took his friend Miss Fenwick to see them. "The remembrances of his youth", she writes, "seemed all pleasant to him...he showed us how he drew his bed to the door, that he might see the top of the window in Trinity College Chapel under which stands that glorious statue of Sir Isaac Newton." She thought them one of the meanest and most dismal apartments in the whole University. But "here", said he, "I was as joyous as a lark".

His first few days were passed in a round of excitement, vividly described in *The Prelude*:

> Questions, directions, warnings and advice
> Flowed in upon me, from all sides.

May we suppose that *Ten Minutes Advice to Freshmen*, printed in 1785, was in his hands—a little work resembling our Freshers' "Don't"? Its wise counsel on the care of money and time, and on general behaviour, was perhaps lightly skimmed. But there were practical hints concerning clubs, dress, amusements, and not least, tips—to bedmakers, shoe-cleaners, coal-porters, hairdressers. Undergraduates in those days paid a good deal of attention to dress. White waistcoats and white silk stockings were worn in Hall. Some wore powder. Wordsworth speaks of himself as attired in splendid clothes, with hose of silk and hair glittering like rimy trees. They carried their gown, a sleeveless gown, called a curtain, tucked up under their arm. Dorothy, after her first visit to William, wrote "it looked so odd to see smart powdered heads with black caps like helmets,...but I assure you...it is exceedingly becoming".

Even in so large a College as St John's there were probably not as many as 150 undergraduates in residence at any one time. They were a very varied body of men. No College did more for the poor man, and, save Trinity, none drew so many of rank and fashion, but it was the growing middle class that was mainly represented. A man was admitted as either a nobleman, a Fellow Commoner, a pensioner, or a sizar. The annual entry at the time consisted of about thirty pensioners, ten or eleven sizars, six or seven Fellow Commoners, and occasionally one or two noblemen.

Fellow Commoners were usually of the same age as other under-graduates; they belonged to county families or were the sons of rich business men. They dined with the Fellows at the High Table. Most of them were wealthy and could afford to be idle. They were supposed to take lectures and examinations, but these rules were not regularly enforced. They wore a gold-laced gown and gold tassel to their cap. Among them doubtless were Wordsworth's "chattering popinjays".

Of the pensioners many were sons of clergy and professional men who had their living to earn and wanted to get a fellowship as a good start. The sizars had once been virtually servants, brought up to the University by richer men, and in return for their services gaining the opportunity of study and advancement. But this had changed. The last of their menial duties, waiting in Hall, had just been abolished (1786). A sizarship was becoming more like an entrance scholarship. It was a useful institution, for it was not an award, tied to school or county, like the scholarships and fellowships, but a status. A poor boy, by entering as a sizar, could get much reduced terms.

The men came from a great variety of schools, large and small, or from private tutors. North country schools, particularly Sedbergh and Beverley, and Wordsworth's own school, Hawkshead, an Elizabethan foundation, were prominent; of others, Eton, West-minster, Canterbury, Shrewsbury, Charterhouse and Harrow seem the most common. A few men came from the West Indies and the American colonies, sons of planters, generally to read for the Bar. The great majority took holy orders. Others entered politics, law and the army, or returned to country life, while a few became physi-cians, and one or two went into industry.

Amongst Wordsworth's contemporaries were many interesting men, some destined to high position. Castlereagh overlapped him by a term; there was a grandson of Lord Bute, who went into the East India Company's service; Wellington's younger brother, Gerald, later a canon of St Paul's (the Iron Duke would not make him a bishop); a future Primus of the Scottish Episcopal Church;

a future Chief Justice of Jamaica; Philip Francis, son of the reputed author of the *Letters of Junius*; two great linguists, John Kelly, the Celtic scholar, and John Palmer of Cockermouth, later Professor of Arabic, a very reserved man—it was said of him that he could be silent in more languages than anyone else in Europe—and the young Heberden, already showing his father's distinction. Amongst those who were to win fame in the long wars were Daniel Hoghton, commemorated by Chantrey in St Paul's, who fell at Albuera; George Gordon, the last of the Dukes of Gordon, who became a general, and is the hero of the famous song, "O where, tell me where, is your Highland laddie gone", and Alexander John Scott, Nelson's private secretary, who was on the *Victory* at Trafalgar. William's outlook widened in this company; when he went up he had been thinking only of the Church or Law, after he came down he felt he could make a soldier or a journalist.

Though in eighteenth-century Cambridge the junior members of a College were broadly divided into gentlemen of fortune and poor scholars, and men of course formed their own sets, there is no suggestion in *The Prelude* of class barriers in College life—rather the contrary; and we need not think it a leading feature. Byron, for example, said of his contemporary Kirke White, a sizar at St John's, "for my own part I should have been very proud of such an acquaintance". Young men of talent soon made their mark. Wordsworth entered at once and fully into the social life of the College. "The weeks went roundly on with invitations, suppers, wine and fruit".

> If a throng was near
> That way I leaned by nature; for my heart
> Was social, and loved idleness and joy.

In a few lines of the *Prelude* he summarizes the easygoing round of his first year:

> Companionships,
> Friendships, acquaintances, were welcome all.
> We sauntered, played, or rioted; we talked
> Unprofitable talk at morning hours;
> Drifted about along the streets and walks,
> Read lazily in trivial books, went forth
> To gallop through the country in blind zeal
> Of senseless horsemanship, or on the breast
> Of Cam sailed boisterously.

We need add nothing to this.

Within the larger circle was a smaller one, including his cousin Myers, who had come up with him. Their names are together in the Matriculation Register of the University and again when they took their degree three years later. Myers went to the Bar. Wordsworth calls him "a patriot of unabated energy"—he had caught the tone of the College. Other friends were William Terrot, admitted a scholar on the same day as Wordsworth, who became a naval chaplain, Robert Jones, his companion in the memorable walking-tour in France, "the best tempered creature imaginable", wrote Wordsworth, "our long friendship was never subject to a moment's interruption", and John Fleming, two years his senior, from his old school, the "friend then passionately loved". And there were three Pembroke men, Raincock, Second Wrangler of his year (1790), Thomas Middleton, from Christ's Hospital, who became the first Bishop of Calcutta, and William Matthews, son of a London bookseller and Methodist local preacher. Wordsworth later expresses his advanced opinions more freely to Matthews than to anyone else, as they had doubtless done at Cambridge: "I am of that odious class of men called democrats and of that class I shall ever continue." Wordsworth's fondness for walking was notorious in this circle; writing to Matthews he describes himself as "on foot, as you will naturally suppose". But none of these shared the deeper experiences through which in solitary hours his mind was passing. If only he and Coleridge had met at Cambridge, he afterwards lamented, he would have been less alone.

Of his Johnian friends, Fleming and Terrot seem to have been hard reading men. But not a third of the men who matriculated with him went out in Honours and quite a number went down without graduating.

The College routine began with early morning chapel usually at 7. From 9 to 12.30 were lecture hours. Lectures were given in the Hall or the tutor's rooms; themes for the Rhetoric lecturer were read in the Chapel. We see the tutor's room—"all studded round, as thick as chairs could stand, with loyal students faithful to their books, half-and-half idlers, hardy recusants and honest dunces". Lectures no doubt varied. Gunning writes: "Nothing could be pleasanter than the hour passed at Seale's lectures." Wordsworth, young as he was, found himself a year ahead of his contemporaries. This he afterwards said had been unlucky for him. I "got into rather an idle way; reading nothing but classic authors according to my fancy and Italian poetry".

After lectures followed a visit to the hairdresser and dinner at 1.30 or 2. There was no organized sport; riding and river parties were the principal amusements, and the afternoon passed in calls on friends and tea, coffee or chocolate at a coffee-house with the papers. Evening chapel followed and at 8 the bedmaker called to enquire about supper, bringing a bill of fare. Several men would join together in a supper or wine party.

Men of the same school or county formed clubs: the freshman's guide calls them "useless things", "more easily got into than out of". Some formed literary societies. Christopher Wordsworth, his younger brother, when at Trinity, records in his diary: "The Society this evening met at my rooms....Time before supper was spent in hearing Coleridge repeat some original poetry (he having neglected to write his essay, which therefore is to be produced next week)."

Not all men passed their lives so blamelessly. Gunning considered the late 'seventies and 'eighties as the worst part of our history. Reformers pointed to the extravagance and indiscipline of the University. In a Town and Gown row in March 1788 a drayman was killed and two undergraduates were charged with murder but acquitted. College orders tell a similar tale. One threatens with rustication any person detected in breaking the door of another. The scholars' cook in 1790 was fined the next three-quarters of his salary for giving undue credit to the men. Wordsworth later spoke of the frantic and dissolute manners of that time. The source of the trouble was the presence of a class of man with plenty of money and no obligation to do anything. So long as this class was numerous and ill restrained, order and work were not likely to prevail, and incidents occurred which were a scandal to the University.

But though there was a prevailing tone of idleness, the reading men undoubtedly worked hard. The competition for University honours was keen. High places in examinations were not won without effort. Christopher Wordsworth tells us that from September to December before his examination he read $9\frac{3}{4}$ hours a day. Chief Justice Denman, who was here in the 1790's, said that he worked all day and played chess in the evenings. If Fellow Commoners occasionally worked, sizars and the poorer pensioners worked a great deal harder.

Of the senior members of the College Wordsworth formed no favourable opinion.

The Master, Chevallier, died in 1789. Wordsworth tells us that according to custom the coffin was brought into the Hall and the pall was "stuck over by copies of verses English or Latin, the composition of the students of St John's. My uncle seemed mortified when upon enquiry he learnt that none of these verses were from my pen, 'because', said he, 'it would have been a fair opportunity for distinguishing yourself'. I did not, however, regret that I had been silent on this occasion, as I felt no interest in the deceased person, with whom I had had no intercourse and whom I had never seen but during his walks in the College grounds."

Of the Fellows, who at the time numbered fifty-five, all but four were required to take holy orders, so that the High Table was for the most part a clerical body. The younger Fellows were men in the early or middle twenties; they joined in the parties and amusements of the richer undergraduates. The abler of them in due course attained to College office. As a body, the Fellows were not what we should call old, for they held office generally only for a short time, while waiting for a College living or other promotion. There were not many College offices and for some of the Fellows the life was one of enforced idleness. Among them, there were doubtless queer characters; Edward Christian, for example, who had perhaps just reached what Gunning wittily calls "the full vigour of his incapacity"—not to mention one or two old men whose infirmities disqualified them even from the seniority. The government of the College by the eight seniors left too much to chance, though actually in Wordsworth's time the seniority included some men of parts.

To the official Fellows Wordsworth did not take kindly:

> men whose sway
> And known authority of office served
> To set our minds on edge, and did no more.

What unpleasant experiences this refers to we do not know. College rules were doubtless irksome and the means of enforcement, by impositions, savoured of school rather than College life. But if Frewen was as grim as this he must soon have forgotten the jolly days when he and Uncle William had idled with that rich and agreeable Fellow Commoner William Wilberforce. As he was now contemplating matrimony and retiring to a College living, he may have become less attentive to his pupils.

In December 1803 Wordsworth wrote to his brother Richard:

> I have just received an application for a debt of £10. 15s. 3½d. from my College Tutor for my expenses at the University. I wish it to be paid, as indeed it ought to have been many years ago....Direct the money to the Revd James Wood, St John's, Cambridge.

This was nearly thirteen years after he had left College. Tutorial Bursars need never despair.

He had been transferred to Dr James Wood, one of the most interesting men of the time. The son of a weaver, very poor, he had rooms called the Tub on O, Second Court, reached by a trap-door in the floor, of which he was the last occupant. (It was a pity Miss Fenwick did not see these.) He was a man of high character, reckoned the foremost mathematician in the University, and in due course became Master. But he may very well have been a strict tutor—as Vice-Chancellor, later, he was to suppress the debates of the Union Society.

To judge from the state of discipline in the University the office of Dean was probably not a sinecure. The Senior Dean, Thomas Cockshutt, was the son of an ironmaster, a man of thirty-seven, and a mathematician like most of the College officials. The little we know of him shows him as able, disinterested and broad-minded. He saved the young Scott from rustication for neglect of mathematics, contending that this was due not to idleness but to the fact that his real interest was literature. Benjamin Holmes, the Junior Dean, was not perhaps as easygoing as he became in later life, when he had retired to the Rectory of Freshwater in the Isle of Wight. Rumour had it that a good deal of contraband reposed in the Rectory buildings. Clearly he had learned to turn a blind eye to some things.

None of his teachers seems to have made any impression on Wordsworth with the exception of William Taylor, Master of the Hawkshead School, who had encouraged his first attempts at poetry. As his later writings show, he was not appreciative of the guidance of a more experienced mind. "Love nature and books", he wrote later to an undergraduate, "seek these and you will be happy."

To the great disappointment of Uncle William, and the doubts even of the devoted Dorothy, he gave up the idea of academic honours. He could not endure to drudge at mathematics, the main road to distinction, and he strongly disliked the competitive spirit in the mathematical tripos. A very little reading would suffice for a pass degree and with this he determined to be satisfied. Moods, vague reading and good-natured lounging filled up more of the map of his collegiate life. At St John's there were examinations twice a year and themes had to be given in regularly to the Rhetoric lecturer. These things became the "forced labour, now and then," of which he speaks.

In the examinations, in his first term he was placed in the first class, in the following June in the second class; in his second and third year examinations, he was not classed, as he did not take the whole examination, but he is twice reported as showing "considerable merit" in the subjects which he took and once as distinguished in the Classic.

"Look was there none within these walls to shame my easy spirits", he wrote in the *Prelude*. Had he forgotten, or never bothered to read, the reports of the examiners—for their language is not only monitory, but positively menacing, to easygoing spirits.

He had misgivings; he saw crowds of his inferiors glorified around him, his schoolfellows becoming high Wranglers and Fellows of Colleges, while he seemed to be achieving nothing. Often afterwards he regretted it; in some moods he blamed the place and the people— the University, the College, had borne no resemblance to his schoolboy dreams, but at the last he blamed himself. Yet he was certainly not alone in his dislike and criticism of the narrow academic curriculum in Cambridge at the time. Other men did the same as he for the same reason. Denman, for example, and George Tennyson, the Poet Laureate's father, of the same year at St John's, both took a pass degree from dislike of Mathematics. And Wordsworth, though reading cursorily, read widely in several languages and literatures. The heroic voice that defended liberty through so many terrible years found its inspiration there.

What had Cambridge meant to him? The official body little indeed—he had been "to himself a guide". And from the round of academic study he detached himself in proud rebellion.

He describes himself aptly as "ill-tutored for captivity", and of two compulsory features of College life, the Lecture Room and Chapel, one he found barren, the other a mockery. But the living society and the spiritual presences were new and powerful forces— the associations and friendships had meant a great deal—

> So many happy youths, so wide and fair
> A congregation in its budding-time
> Of health and hope and beauty.

The precincts, the grounds, the enclosures old, the noble dead, whose presence haunted them—Milton's rooms, Newton's statue, Spenser's and Chaucer's memory: these were influences to penetrate and disturb the mind—all that sense of the past which is ever present in a place of great tradition. And the liberal views and democratic temper of the young men joined with his natural disposition and upbringing to prepare him for his eager reception of revolutionary ideas. Not least, he had been happy—"This was a gladsome time"— left alone to move on a stage further in the discovery of himself. Cambridge might have done worse for him had it tried to do more.

He took his degree in January 1791 and went down without prospects or plan, his mind clouded by the uncertainties of the future. When, two years later, he published his first poems, he wrote: "As I had done nothing by which to distinguish myself at the University, I thought these little things might show that I could do something." He was right; the wayward and disappointing undergraduate was the most original genius of his time.

*   *   *   *

The Master's address had obviously been much enjoyed; his humorous references to Cambridge life then and now had met with appreciative response, and he was greeted with warm applause at the end. And with the details of Wordsworth's habits and environment fresh in our mind, we next heard a reading of selected poetry and prose by Wordsworth, his critics and his parodists, with a commentary; the reading of passages was done alternately by John Wilders (*A*) and Peter Croft (*B*).

*   *   *   *

READING AND COMMENTARY

A. It would be very nice to be able to believe that the time Wordsworth saved from academic work had been spent in writing poetry—if that mute, inglorious third year had been redeemed by something immortal. But there's nothing to justify us in believing anything of the kind. He wrote some verses, certainly, but they were a very long way indeed from being poetry—they were certainly not yet in any way original. Here's one of them, *Lines written while Sailing in a Boat at Evening*:

B.   How richly glows the water's breast
    Before us, ting'd with evening hues,
   While, facing thus the crimson west,
    The boat her silent course pursues!
   And see how dark the backward stream!
    A little moment past so smiling!
   And still, perhaps, with faithless gleam,
    Some other loiterers beguiling.

   Such views the youthful Bard allure;
    But, heedless of the following gloom,
   He deems their colours shall endure
    Till peace go with him to the tomb.
   —And let him nurse his fond deceit,
    And what if he must die in sorrow!
   Who would not cherish dreams so sweet,
    Though grief and pain must come to-morrow!

A. If that poem is typical of the things he was thinking about while he was up here, then he must have been very much like any other undergraduate with literary ambitions—spending a good deal of time wondering whether he was going to be a good poet or not, and whether the game was really worth the candle. Just worrying about poetry, in fact—not being in any sense a poet. And in Wordsworth, this doubt and hesitation was very deeply rooted indeed. It was many years before he began to feel really certain of himself. But Cambridge did contribute something towards this certainty. It helped him to become familiar with books, and even more, to live where so many great men in the past had lived. Later, he wrote about this encouragement like this:

B.   Those were the days
        Which first encouraged me to trust
        With firmness, hitherto but lightly touch'd
        With such a daring thought, that I might leave
        Some monument behind me which pure hearts
        Should reverence. The instinctive humbleness
        Upheld even by the very name and thought
        Of printed books and authorship, began
        To melt away, and further, the dread awe
        Of mighty names was softened down, and seem'd
        Approachable, admitting fellowship
        Of modest sympathy.

A.   This mood of self-doubt—the fear that poets can only hope to enjoy the short glow of that sunset he'd described while sailing on the river, and that their end is in grief and pain—it was many years before he got rid of such thoughts and moods. If, indeed, he was ever quite free from them. But the struggle to free himself from them, and to reach up to a more stable and happy frame of mind, was the driving force of much of his best poetry. For example, there's a poem which HE called *Resolution and Independence*—but it's more familiarly known as *The Leech-gatherer*. He wrote it in 1802, and its main subject is exactly the same as those lines written sailing on the Cam. But by that time, he was no longer writing verses. He had become a poet, and of a completely original kind.

Before we read this poem, I'd like to remind you of one of the great influences that came into his life after he left Cambridge—his sister Dorothy. It so happens that in her *Journal*, she has described the very same incident that Wordsworth used for his poem. Here it is:

B.   "When William and I returned from accompanying Jones, we met an old man almost double. He had on a coat, thrown over his shoulders, above his waistcoat and coat. Under this he carried a bundle, and had an apron on and a night-cap. His face was interesting. He had dark eyes and a long nose. He was of Scotch parents, but had been born in the army. He had had a wife, and 'she was a good woman, and it pleased God to bless us with ten children'. All these were dead but one, of whom he had not heard for many years, a sailor. His trade was to gather leeches, but now leeches are scarce, and he had not strength for it. He said leeches were very scarce, partly owing to this dry season, but many years they have been scarce. He supposed it owing to their having been much sought after, that they did not breed fast, and were of slow growth. Leeches were formerly two and six per hundred; they are now thirty shillings. It was then late in the evening, when the light was just going away."

A   And now, here is what Wordsworth makes of the same incident:

> There was a roaring in the wind all night;
> The rain came heavily and fell in floods;
> But now the sun is rising calm and bright;
> The birds are singing in the distant woods;
> Over his own sweet voice the Stock-dove broods;
> The Jay makes answer as the Magpie chatters;
> And all the air is filled with pleasant noise of waters.
>
> All things that love the sun are out of doors;
> The sky rejoices in the morning's birth;
> The grass is bright with rain-drops;—on the moors
> The hare is running races in her mirth;
> And with her feet she from the plashy earth
> Raises a mist; that, glittering in the sun,
> Runs with her all the way, wherever *she* doth run.
>
> *I* was a Traveller then upon the moor;
> I saw the hare that raced about with joy;
> I heard the woods and distant waters roar;
> Or heard them not, as happy as a boy;
> But, as it sometimes chanceth, from the might
> Of joy in minds that can no further go,
> As high as we have mounted in delight
> In our dejection do we sink as low;
> To me that morning did it happen so;
> And fears and fancies thick upon me came;
> Dim sadness—and blind thoughts, I knew not, nor could name.
>
> I heard the sky-lark warbling in the sky;
> And I bethought me of the playful hare:
> Even such a happy Child of earth am I;
> Even as those blissful creatures do I fare;
> Far from the world I walk, and from all care;
> But there may come another day to me—
> Solitude, pain of heart, distress and poverty.

My whole life have I lived in pleasant thought,
As if life's business were a summer mood;
As if all needful things would come unsought
To genial faith, still rich in genial good;
But how can He expect that others should
Build for him, sow for him, and at his call
Love him, who for himself will take no heed at all?

I thought of Chatterton, the marvellous boy,
The sleepless Soul that perished in his pride;
Of Him who walked in glory and in joy
Following his plough, along the mountain-side:
By our own spirits are we deified:
We Poets, in our youth begin in gladness;
But thereof come in the end despondency and madness.

B.   Now, whether it were by a peculiar grace,
A leading from above, a something given,
Yet it befell that, in this lonely place,
When I with these untoward thoughts had striven,
Beside a pool bare to the eye of heaven
I saw a Man before me unawares:
The oldest man he seemed that ever wore grey hairs.

As a huge stone is sometimes seen to lie
Couched on the bald top of an eminence;
Wonder to all who do the same espy,
By what means it could thither come, and whence;
So that it seemed a thing endued with sense:
Like a sea-beast crawled forth, that on a shelf
Of rock or sand reposeth, there to sun itself;

Such seemed this Man, not all alive nor dead,
Nor all asleep—in his extreme old age:
His body was bent double, feet and head
Coming together in life's pilgrimage;
As if some dire constraint of pain, or rage
Of sickness felt by him in times long past,
A more than human weight upon his frame had cast.

Himself he propped, limbs, body, and pale face,
Upon a long grey staff of shaven wood:
And, still as I drew near with gentle pace,
Upon the margin of that moorish flood
Motionless as a cloud the old Man stood,
That heareth not the loud winds when they call;
And moveth all together, if it move at all.

At length, himself unsettling, he the pond
Stirred with his staff, and fixedly did look
Upon the muddy water, which he conned,
As if he had been reading in a book:
And now a stranger's privilege I took,
And drawing to his side, to him did say,
"This morning gives us promise of a glorious day."

A.   A gentle answer did the old Man make,
In courteous speech which forth he slowly drew:
And him with further words I thus bespake,
"What occupation do you there pursue?
This is a lonesome place for one like you."
Ere he replied, a flash of mild surprise
Broke from the sable orbs of his yet-vivid eyes.

His words came feebly, from a feeble chest,
But each in solemn order followed each,
With something of a lofty utterance drest—
Choice word and measured phrase, above the reach
Of ordinary men; a stately speech;
Such as grave Livers do in Scotland use,
Religious men, who give to God and man their dues.

He told, that to these waters he had come
To gather leeches, being old and poor:
Employment hazardous and wearisome!
And he had many hardships to endure:
From pond to pond he roamed, from moor to moor;
Housing, with God's good help, by choice or chance;
And in this way he gained an honest maintenance.

B.   The old Man stood talking by my side;
But now his voice to me was like a stream
Scarce heard; nor word from word could I divide;
And the whole body of the Man did seem
Like one whom I had met with in a dream;
Or like a man from some far region sent,
To give me human strength, by apt admonishment.

My former thoughts returned: the fear that kills;
And hope that is unwilling to be fed;
Cold, pain, and labour, and all fleshly ills;
And mighty Poets in their misery dead.
—Perplexed, and longing to be comforted,
My question eagerly I did renew,
"How is it that you live, and what is it you do?"

A.   He with a smile did then his words repeat;
And said that, gathering leeches, far and wide
He travelled; stirring thus about his feet
The waters of the pools where they abide.
"Once I could meet with them on every side;
But they have dwindled long by slow decay;
Yet still I persevere, and find them where I may."

While he was talking thus, the lonely place,
The old Man's shape, and speech—all troubled me:
In my mind's eye I seemed to see him pace
About the weary moors continually,
Wandering about alone and silently.
While I these thoughts within myself pursued,
He, having made a pause, the same discourse renewed.

And soon with this he other matter blended,
Cheerfully uttered, with demeanour kind,
But stately in the main; and, when he ended,
I could have laughed myself to scorn to find
In that decrepit Man so firm a Mind.
"God," said I, "be my help and stay secure;
I'll think of the Leech-gatherer on the lonely moor!"

B.   Well, that is an example of his poetry at its most Words-worthian—completely original, unlike anything that had been written before, and very seldom imitated since with much success. It's a kind of poetry that Wordsworth described very clearly himself, in the Preface he wrote to the volume in which the *Leech-gatherer* was published:

A.   "The principal object proposed in these poems was to choose incidents and situations from common life, and to relate or describe them, throughout, as far as was possible in a selection of the language really used by men, and, at the same time, to throw over them a certain colouring of imagination, whereby ordinary things should be presented to the mind in an unusual aspect; and further, and above all, to make these incidents and situations interesting by tracing in them, truly though not ostentatiously, the primary laws of our nature."

B.   But it's a very dangerous kind of poetry—it walks on a knife-edge between success and failure. A little weakening in the force of imagination, a trifle too much ostentation in the morality, and the sublime becomes ridiculous. The poem we've just read was taken in the right way by some of Wordsworth's friends—Charles Lamb, Coleridge, and Southey. But to many of the reviewers it seemed to have fallen very far on the wrong side. Here is a specimen of the kind of criticism that Wordsworth encountered in his own day:

A. "Their peculiarities of diction alone, are enough to render them ridiculous; but the author before us really seems anxious to court this literary martyrdom by a device still more infallible,—we mean, that of connecting his most lofty, tender, or impassioned conceptions, with objects and incidents, which the greater part of his readers will probably persist in thinking low, silly, or uninteresting. It is possible enough, we allow, that the sight of a friend's spade, or a sparrow's nest, or a man gathering leeches, might really have suggested to a mind like his a train of powerful impressions and interesting reflections; but it is certain, that to most minds, such associations will always appear forced, strained and unnatural; and that the composition in which it is attempted to exhibit them, will always have the air of parody, or ludicrous and affected singularity."

B. Curiously right as a prophecy, anyhow—for Wordsworth has always provoked a great deal of parody. Some of it quite friendly parody—more a sign of affection than disapproval. I'd put in that class "The White Knight's Song", from *Alice Through the Looking Glass*—it's not exactly a parody of the *Leech-gatherer*—but with that in mind, you'll have little doubt what Lewis Carroll was up to. Let me remind you of it:

A.　　　　"I'll tell thee everything I can:
　　　　　　There's little to relate.
　　　　　I saw an aged aged man,
　　　　　　A-sitting on a gate.
　　　　　'Who are you, aged man?' I said.
　　　　　　'And how is it you live?'
　　　　　And his answer trickled through my head
　　　　　　Like water through a sieve.

　　　　　He said 'I look for butterflies
　　　　　　That sleep among the wheat:
　　　　　I make them into mutton-pies,
　　　　　　And sell them in the street.
　　　　　I sell them unto men,' he said,
　　　　　　'Who sail upon the seas;
　　　　　And that's the way I get my bread—
　　　　　　A trifle, if you please.'

But I was thinking of a way
  To feed oneself on batter,
And so go on from day to day
  Getting a little fatter.

I shook him well from side to side,
  Until his face was blue:
'Come, tell me how you live,' I cried,
  'And what it is you do!'

He said 'I hunt for haddock's eyes
  Among the heather bright,
And work them into waistcoat buttons,
  In the silent night.'

B.   And now, if e'er by chance I put
  My fingers into glue,
Or madly squeeze a right-hand foot
  Into a left-hand shoe,
Or if I drop upon my toe
  A very heavy weight,
I weep, for it reminds me so
Of that old man I used to know—
Whose look was mild, whose speech was slow,
Whose hair was whiter than the snow,
Whose face was very like a crow,
With eyes, like cinders, all aglow,
Who seemed distracted with his woe,
Who rocked his body to and fro,
And muttered mumblingly and low,
As if his mouth were full of dough,
Who snorted like a buffalo—
That summer evening long ago
A-sitting on a gate."

A.   Fair criticism, perhaps—at any rate kindly criticism, not out-
rageous and bitter, like so much of the criticism he had to suffer in
his lifetime. There's another notable parody of Wordsworth, by
James Kennedy Stephen, once President of the Union, Fellow of
King's. It states very fairly and very well the distinction that must
be made between Wordsworth at his best, and Wordsworth below
his best. And unfortunately there's no use denying that he made
things more difficult for his readers, both then and now, by writing
a great *deal* below his best. But before hearing Stephen's sonnet,
here is the original he had in mind. It's one of the best-known of

Wordsworth's political sonnets, *Thoughts of a Briton on the Subjugation of Switzerland*:

B.   Two voices are there; one is of the sea,
         One of the mountains; each a mighty voice;
         In both from age to age thou didst rejoice,
         They were the chosen music, Liberty!
         There came a Tyrant, and with holy glee
         Thou fought'st against him; but hast vainly striven:
         Thou from thy Alpine holds at length art driven,
         Where not a torrent murmurs heard by thee.
         Then cleave, O cleave to that which still is left;
         For, high-souled Maid, what sorrow would it be
         That Mountain floods should thunder as before,
         And Ocean bellow from his rocky shore,
         And neither awful Voice be heard by thee!

A. Now here is Stephen's sonnet:

         "Two voices are there: one is of the deep;
         It learns the storm-cloud's thunderous melody,
         Now roars, now murmurs with the changing sea,
         Now bird-like pipes, now closes soft in sleep;
         And one is of an old half-witted sheep
         Which bleats articulate monotony,
         And indicates that two and one are three,
         That grass is green, lakes damp, and mountains steep:
         And, Wordsworth, both are thine: at certain times
         Forth from the heart of thy melodious rhymes,
         The form and pressure of high thoughts will burst:
         At other times—good Lord, I'd rather be
         Quite unacquainted with the ABC
         Than write such hopeless rubbish as thy worst."

B. It's always been easy to make fun of Wordsworth at his worst—and perhaps that's why his purely literary reputation has often been a little unsteady—perhaps why he has been liable to periods of neglect, if not disparagement. But after all, he himself in his calmer moods cared very little for purely literary reputation. As Dorothy Wordsworth once wrote: "I am sure it will be very long before the poems have an extensive sale. Nay, it will not be while he is alive to know it. God be thanked, William has no mortification on this head, and I may safely say that those who are connected with him have not an atom of that species of disappointment. We have too rooted a confidence in the purity of his intentions, and the power with which they are executed. His writings will live, will comfort the afflicted, and animate the happy to purer happiness; when we, and our little cares, are all forgotten."

A. And that is very much what happened. Of the many tributes to Wordsworth's power to comfort afflicted minds, here is just one, by John Stuart Mill. In his *Autobiography*, he tells how, round about 1828, he had sunk into a deep depression. Convinced in theory that the world ought to be, and could be, in many ways reformed, he was haunted by the idea that even in a reformed world, men might after all not be happy. And then he goes on:

"What made Wordsworth's poems a medicine for my state of mind, was that they expressed not mere outward beauty, but states of feeling, and thought coloured by feeling, under the excitement of beauty. They seemed to be the very culture of the feelings, which I was in quest of. In them I seemed to draw from a source of inward joy, of sympathetic and imaginative pleasure, which could be shared in by all human beings, which had no connection with struggle or imperfection, but would be made richer by every improvement in the physical or social condition of mankind. From them I seemed to learn what would be the perennial sources of happiness when all the greater evils of life shall have been removed. And I felt myself at once better and happier as I came under their influence."

B. Mill doesn't tell us what poems especially helped him, but the two sonnets with which we are going to end must surely have been among them. First, the sonnet composed upon Westminster Bridge, 3 September 1802:

A.   Earth has not anything to show more fair;
            Dull would he be of soul who could pass by
            A sight so touching in its majesty:
            This City now doth, like a garment, wear
            The beauty of the morning; silent, bare,
            Ships, towers, domes, theatres, and temples lie
            Open unto the fields, and to the sky;
            All bright and glittering in the smokeless air.
            Never did sun more beautifully steep
            In his first splendour, valley, rock, or hill;
            Ne'er saw I, never felt, a calm so deep!
            The river glideth at his own sweet will:
            Dear God! the very houses seem asleep;
            And all that mighty heart is lying still.

B.   The world is too much with us: late and soon,
         Getting and spending, we lay waste our powers:
         Little we see in Nature that is ours;
         We have given our hearts away, a sordid boon!
         This Sea that bares her bosom to the moon;
         The winds that will be howling at all hours,
         And are up-gathered now like sleeping flowers;
         For this, for everything we are out of tune;
         It moves us not.—Great God, I'd rather be
         A Pagan suckled in a creed outworn;
         So might I, standing on this pleasant lea,
         Have glimpses that would make me less forlorn;
         Have sight of Proteus rising from the sea;
         Or hear old Triton blow his wreathed horn.

                    *   *   *   *

Again, the readings were very much enjoyed, and although at times perhaps the parodies seemed to excite more interest than their originals, the excellent quality of the recitations made the most of even the admitted mediocrities, and did full justice to the master-pieces. After the readings the company adjourned to Hall, and had lunch.

There were only two toasts; first, THE KING, proposed by the Master; and, second, WORDSWORTH, proposed by the Master of Trinity.

                    *   *   *   *

THE TOAST: "WORDSWORTH", BY THE MASTER OF TRINITY

When I heard that the Master was to read us a paper in your beautiful Combination Room, on St John's in Wordsworth's undergraduate days, I felt sure we should hear something of historical interest and value. Nor have we been disappointed. The Master's knowledge, not only of the bygone customs of the College, but of so many of its personalities, both dons and undergraduates of that day, has been of great interest to us all.

And the second part of the programme both edified and enter-tained us. It is a great thing to be able to laugh at those you love, when you can do it as well as Lewis Carroll and J. K. S. The greatest Wordsworthian I ever knew well, Edward Grey of Fallodon, liked a joke about the bard. I remember his delight over Wordsworth's phrase "the solemn bleat" of a sheep. He said to me, "No one but downright old Daddy Wordsworth would ever have talked of a 'solemn bleat'".

It was with pride and pleasure that I received your invitation to propose this toast, on this occasion and in this place. I hope the historic rivalry of John's and Trinity will never cease. For four hundred years its fortunes have swayed to and fro, but John's never scored a bigger point (not even in the Boat Race against Oxford in 1950) than when, practically in one undergraduate generation, it produced three such men as Wilberforce, Castlereagh and Wordsworth, to say nothing of Palmerston a decade later.

There were many faults in eighteenth-century England, and very many in eighteenth-century Cambridge, but could our reformed and regimented era produce such a quaternion of men? Of the four, the dearest to our hearts are Wordsworth and Wilberforce, and Wordsworth above all reigns not only in the hearts but in the minds of our perturbed and disillusioned generation, more even than Tennyson of Trinity and far more than Byron. Through Wordsworth alone, many of us can sometimes find that

> Central peace, subsisting at the heart
> Of endless agitation.

Your claim on Wordsworth can be disputed by no one else in Cambridge. Pembroke and Peterhouse have each a share in Gray; you sowed Bentley and we reaped him. But as to Wordsworth there is nothing to be added to his statement:

> The Evangelist St John my patron was.

Presumably, therefore, he was referring in part to certain Fellows of John's when he wrote of the "grave elders, men unscoured, grotesque". This description by no means applies to all the Fellows of John's at that period—not even to all the Elders. And we learn from Gunning and other authentic sources that there were Fellows of Trinity to whom the description would equally well have applied in the days when Wordsworth and his undergraduate friends looked round for sources of mirth.

Nevertheless, the 1780's were the nadir of donhood in England. It was the darkness before the dawn. But the undergraduate society which mattered much more to young William, won from him a noble eulogy in *The Prelude*:

> nor was it least
> Of many benefits, in later years
> Derived from academic institutes
> And rules, that they held something up to view
> Of a Republic, where all stood thus far
> Upon equal ground; that we were brothers all

In honour, as in one community,
Scholars and gentlemen; where, furthermore,
Distinction open lay to all that came,
And wealth and titles were in less esteem
Than talents, worth and prosperous industry.

It is clear from what Wordsworth tells us of his uneventful life at John's, that it was just what he then required. The spiritual powers that had been planted in him in his boyhood among the Lake mountains, were here allowed quietly to germinate in a friendly and studious soil, until he had acquired the strength to go forth and endure the fierce experiences of passion and disillusionment through which he passed in France and London from 1791 to 1795, before he found his true self and Coleridge and Grasmere.

Nor was he entirely without benefit from the peculiar studies of the Cambridge of that date. It is true that he shrank from the drudgery of mathematical study, but Wordsworth tells us that "mathematics and geometric truth" had their part in forming his mind and soul. They were restful to his spirit by imparting

a sense
Of permanent and universal sway
And paramount belief.

He put Newton alongside of Shakespeare and Milton, "labourers divine".

Thus prepared, he went, during the Long Vacation of 1790, with a brother Johnian on the famous walking tour through the Alps, which was one of the formative spiritual events of his life.

Wordsworth was yours and yours alone, yet his fragrant memory forms a friendly link between our Colleges. From his rooms over your kitchens he looked towards Trinity. He tells us how he used to listen to the double chime of "Trinity's loquacious clock", and he has honoured Roubiliac's statue of Newton in our antechapel with words too familiar for quotation.

The windows and the garden of Trinity Lodge command a fine view of the south side of the buildings and "backs" of St John's, so that I often fancy him striding over the older of your two bridges to the grounds beyond the river, then untouched by the Gothic revival, to ruminate apart from his lighter-hearted companions; there he would gaze, entranced by moonlight, on the ivied ash-tree:

Through hours of silence, till the porter's bell,
A punctual follower on the stroke of nine,
Rang with its blunt unceremonious voice
Inexorable summons!

There was, however, one thing at John's which the freedom-loving William did not like—compulsory chapel. There is a very strong passage in *The Prelude* about

> The witless shepherd who persists to drive
> A flock that thirsts not to a pool disliked

and as he left this passage in *The Prelude* to be published after his death in 1850, there is at least a probability that he never changed his mind about it.

I wonder therefore if he ever discussed the vexed question with his brother Christopher, Master of Trinity from 1820 to 1841, whom he visited several times at our Lodge. For the joke is that Christopher Wordsworth, "witless shepherd" indeed, made himself fiercely unpopular by raising the penalties for irregular attendance at Chapel. Was Christopher ever shown the manuscript of *The Prelude*?

William has himself recorded in Book Three of *The Prelude* a famous occasion on which he attended John's Chapel under peculiar circumstances. According to his account he had toasted the memory of Milton so often in the rooms at Christ's, that his brain was "excited by the fumes of wine" for the first and last time in his life. Yet he ran through the streets the whole way back to John's in time to huddle on his surplice and attend Chapel without scandal. As some one said of the incident thus recorded: "The poet's standard of intoxication seems to have been deplorably low."

Valuable as his time at College was to him, he had all the while, as he tells us,

> a strangeness in the mind
> A feeling that I was not for that hour
> Nor for that place.

How indeed could it have been otherwise? Cambridge might have sufficed Gray, and South England sufficed Shakespeare and Milton and Marvell; but Wordsworth lives to us as the poet of the mountains and the wilds, who found and conveyed to us hints of their unfathomable secret.

> Love had he known in huts where poor men lie;
> His daily teachers had been woods and rills,
> The silence that is in the starry sky,
> The sleep that is among the lonely hills.
>
> (*Feast at Brougham Castle*)

The genius of Wordsworth is not dramatic, like Shakespeare's and Browning's, but egocentric. Therefore *The Prelude*, which is about himself, is very much more successful than *The Excursion*, which purports to record the thoughts of several other people; but none of them is clearly distinguished from the others; each is a mouth to utter Wordsworth's doctrine which is given more humanly in *The Prelude*. Indeed I have a great deal of sympathy with Jeffrey's famous exclamation, "This will never do", which referred not to all Wordsworth's poetry but to *The Excursion*. There are many very fine passages in it, but the scheme of the poem was unsuited to his genius. With *The Excursion* "we are indeed emerging from the golden period", as Helen Darbishire says in her Clark Lectures on *The Poet Wordsworth*, which I am glad to say are just being published.

So, too, his interest in Nature is not primarily that of an observer of natural appearances, like Tennyson or Turner—although in fact he *can* observe wonderfully, as when he notices the butterfly hanging on a flower—

> How motionless! not frozen seas
> More motionless!

or the cloud caught on the shoulder of the mountain—

> That heareth not the loud winds when they call
> And moveth all together if it move at all.

But on the whole his poems are not a report on the appearances of Nature, but a report on the effect of Nature upon the emotions of William Wordsworth. And as the effect of Nature on Wordsworth is akin to her effect on ourselves, he has become the prophet and priest of a great company. Especially is this the case in our present age, which has found man very unsatisfactory, and is in several different minds about God. Nature, whatever her secret, is with us as before, and more than ever we seek towards God and man through her.

The common denominator of the spiritual life of our divided and subdivided age is found in the reaction of all our hearts to Nature.

> One impulse from a vernal wood
> May teach you more of man,
> Of moral evil and of good
> Than all the sages can.

This was sometime a paradox, but in a certain sense it has truth, if we consider how very little the sages have been able to teach us.

The peculiar power of the best of Wordsworth's poetry lies, I think, in the combination of qualities usually found apart. I mean language of limpid clarity, yet full of the mystery of hinted meaning; and simplicity of words like a child's, expressing the deepest things of life.

> Behold her, single in the field,
> Yon solitary Highland Lass!
> Reaping and singing by herself;
> Stop here, or gently pass!
> Alone she cuts and binds the grain,
> And sings a melancholy strain;
> O listen! for the Vale profound
> Is overflowing with the sound.
>
> No Nightingale did ever chaunt
> More welcome notes to weary bands
> Of travellers in some shady haunt,
> Among Arabian sands:
> A voice so thrilling ne'er was heard
> In spring-time from the Cuckoo-bird,
> Breaking the silence of the seas
> Among the farthest Hebrides.
>
> Will no one tell me what she sings?—
> Perhaps the plaintive numbers flow
> For old, unhappy, far-off things,
> And battles long ago:
> Or is it some more humble lay,
> Familiar matter of to-day?
> Some natural sorrow, loss, or pain,
> That has been, and may be again!
>
> Whate'er the theme, the Maiden sang
> As if her song could have no ending;
> I saw her singing at her work,
> And o'er the sickle bending;—
> I listened, motionless and still;
> And, as I mounted up the hill,
> The music in my heart I bore,
> Long after it was heard no more.

And we, whether we are mounting up the hill of life or declining on its further side, we bear the music and the comfort of Wordsworth's song in our hearts.

It is a hundred years since his death. It is also a hundred years since his resurrection for us all in the first publication of *The Prelude*.

*   *   *   *

The Master of Trinity's graceful references to the College, his eloquent continuation of the themes begun by our Master, and, above all, perhaps, his intensely moving recitation of *The Solitary*

Reaper, will be long remembered. It brought the main proceedings to a fitting climax. Later, many of the company went into the Library, where an exhibition of Wordsworthiana was on view. All had already been given handsome programmes, containing famous extracts from Wordsworth's poems, and numerous reproductions, which are reprinted in this number of *The Eagle*. We print below an authoritative notice of it by the Librarian of King's College: the exhibition was a fascinating conclusion to a celebration which fittingly expressed our sense of pride and gratitude at sharing our membership of the College with one of the greatest of English poets.

J. L. C.

THE WORDSWORTH EXHIBITION IN
ST JOHN'S COLLEGE LIBRARY*

The centenary of the death of William Wordsworth is the occasion of an exhibition in the library of St John's, which should certainly be seen during the present term, and which provides an excuse, if one were needed, to visit one of the finest libraries of Cambridge, second only to Trinity in splendour, though far less well known to the public at large. The richness and variety of the exhibits are a testimony not only to the generous piety of donors but to the careful watching of the book-market by successive librarians of the College, which aroused the professional envy and respectful admiration of the librarian of another foundation.

Wordsworth was admitted to the College on 6 November 1787, and his subscription in his own hand in the Register of Fellows and Scholars is among the exhibits. From his undergraduate period there is a copy of Martin's *Voyage to St Kilda*, 1753, with his signature (*c.* 1788) on the title-page. His love for his College, universally known from his famous lines in *The Prelude*, is further attested by the inscription which he wrote in a copy of the four-volume *Poetical Works* of 1832:

To the Coll: of St. John Cambridge. These volumes are presented by the Author as a testimony, though inadequate, of his respect and gratitude. Wm. Wordsworth.

It was a lucky windfall which brought the College in 1919 the first four editions of *Lyrical Ballads*, the gift of Miss Emma Hutchinson, great-niece of the poet. The title-page of the first edition of 1798 has indeed the London and not the exceedingly rare Bristol imprint, but the second edition of 1800 (the first appearance of the famous Preface) is a precious copy, bearing the signature of Mary Hutchinson, the poet's future wife.

Other association items include first editions of *The Excursion*, 1814, presented by the author to Agnes Nicholson, of *Poems, chiefly of Early and Late Years*, 1842, given to Elizabeth Cookson, and a copy of the second edition of *The Prelude*, 1851, which Mary Wordsworth gave to the same recipient. Among exhibited manuscripts are the holograph† of the sonnet "To my Portrait Painted by Pickersgill at Rydal Mount For St John's College Cambridge", and

---

* Reprinted by kind permission of the author, and of the Editor of the *Cambridge Review*: the article first appeared in the 6 May number.
† Miss Helen Darbishire has since informed us that only the signature is in Wordsworth's hand.

letters to S. T. Coleridge and Robert Southey, the latter given by a devoted benefactor of the library, the late H. P. W. Gatty, who was also the donor of a book, almost unknown in British collections, the first American edition of *Lyrical Ballads*, published at Philadelphia in two volumes in 1802. Among several relics of the poet must be mentioned the striking life-mask executed by B. R. Haydon.

In the ranks of the printed books three great rarities are missing, *An Evening Walk*, *Descriptive Sketches*, and the Bristol *Lyrical Ballads* of 1798. The first and last of these were kindly lent by Lord Rothschild for the opening of the exhibition: they have now crossed the river again to their fire-proof safe at Merton Hall. The filling of these gaps will set the librarian a pleasant exercise in bibliophily. In the meantime he may with reason be proud of the resources already at his command to honour the memory of the greatest Johnian. A. N. L. MUNBY

ST JOHN'S COLLEGE IN
WORDSWORTH'S TIME

THE COLLEGE EXAMINATIONS, WORDSWORTH'S
FRIENDS, AND SOME OTHER MATTERS

T HE Editors have asked me to supplement a little the account
of the College in Wordsworth's time which I gave in my address
and I am adding therefore notes on several matters to which
only brief reference could be made at the time.

College Examinations

In the College archives is a volume containing copies of almost all
the Examiners' reports on the College examinations from 1770 to
1833. The examinations took place in December and June, and were
held in the Hall. Dr Powell had made it a rule to be present himself;
Chevallier apparently did not, as Wordsworth says in his *Memoirs*
that he had never seen him except walking in the College grounds.
Some part of the examination in early days was evidently oral; in
a report of 1772 we read Atley might have deserved a prize, "if he
had spoke louder, as much of his answers as could be heard was very
good". Printed question papers from the date 1810 are preserved in
the College Library.

In the reports the candidates are arranged in three classes. Only
those candidates who took the whole examination are classed, but
comments on the work of other candidates are sometimes included.
Within each class the men were arranged "according to their order
on the boards". From the nature of the reports it seems clear that
they were put up on the College screens, together with the notice of
the subjects for the next examination. Exhibitions and prizes were
awarded to those who did well in both examinations of the year, and
penalties were threatened and occasionally inflicted on those whose
conduct and work had been particularly unsatisfactory. Prizes were
also awarded for regular attendance in Chapel, but in 1785 this was
changed to "the best readers of the lessons in the Chapel". The
Fellow Commoners were required to take the examination: their
names appear in the reports with the prefix "Mr". Prizes were also
regularly awarded for the greatest number of good themes. Under
a College order of 1775 all men were required to give in at least four
themes a term to the Rhetoric lecturer.

At the end of the report for June 1782 the subjects for the academical year 1782–3 are given as follows:

Subjects for next Exam.		For June 1783
3rd year	Hyd & Opt	Pl & Phys Ast
	Butler	St. Matthew
	Mounteney	2nd Philippic of Cicero
2	6 B. Eucl	Mech[s]
	1 Vol Rutherforth	Locke
	8. 10. 13 Sat Juv	Antigone
1st	1 B. Hor. Ep.	1st & 3rd Eucl.
	Life of Agesil.	Algebra
	Beausobre	Logic
		Agricola

The set books were changed from year to year, but the subjects and scope of the examination seem to have remained the same, and this notice gives a fair view of the work on which the men were engaged during their three years' preparation for the University examination.

A work on Christian Apologetics was usually prescribed for the first year. Beausobre appears to be: *An Introduction to the Reading of the Holy Scriptures intended chiefly for young students in Divinity*. By Messrs Beausobre and L'Enfant, Cambridge, 1779.

With this, in most years, was included three *Sermons on the Evidences of the Gospel* by Dr Doddridge, Northampton, 1770, later published as the *Evidences of Christianity* and long used.

In the examinations which Wordsworth took, or should have taken, we note that in December 1787 the Greek text set was the last book of Xenophon's *Anabasis*. Twenty of the first-year men appear in the first class, including Wordsworth and his friends—Jones, Myers and Terrot; in the second class, there are fifteen; in the third class, seven. This was the examination in which Castlereagh was top of the second year.

In June 1788 the prescribed author is Latin, Tacitus, *de mor. Germ.* Fourteen of the first-year men are in the first class, including Myers; four in the second, including Wordsworth; twelve in the third, including Jones.

In his second-year examinations, for December 1788, the set book was *Oedipus Coloneus*. The report shows ten men, including Myers, in the first class; five, including Terrot, in the second; and three in the third, and continues: "Of those who did not go through the whole of the examination and yet had considerable merit are Wordsworth...." Ten men seem to have taken only part of the examination.

In the June examination (1789) thirteen of the second-year men were in the first class and three were "next but little inferior". "The 3rd class is composed of Myers, Moore and Terrot, the two

last of whom are equal. Gill distinguished himself at the examination in Locke, and Jones and Wordsworth in the Classic." The set
book was Livy XXI.

The neglect by some of the men to prepare themselves for the
examination seems to have brought matters to a head this year, for
the report ends: "The behaviour of those who declared they had
not attended to the subjects of the examination is considered by the
Master and Examiners as highly improper and will in future render
them liable to be degraded to the year before them." This was acted
on in June 1791 when five men, "having shown and avowed their
ignorance of Mechanics", were degraded to the year below them
and "unless they pay attention to all the subjects, their terms will
not be granted".

In December (1789) the Classic was Mounteney, presumably
Mounteney's *Demosthenes de Corona*. But Wordsworth's name does
not appear in the report. Terrot was among those near to the first
class. Myers and Jones "distinguished themselves in the Classic",
and Gill in Butler. The Butler usually set was the *Analogy*. Nothing
indicates the cause of Wordsworth's absence, though it is noteworthy
that many reports contain a reference to men missing the whole or
part of the examination or not doing well in it owing to illness.

In Wordsworth's last examination, June 1790, eight of his year
came out in the first class, four in the second, and two in the third.
"Gawthrop, Stephenson, E. Courthope, Jones, Moore, Myers,
Wordsworth and Hughes are mentioned in the order in which they
stand on the boards and had considerable merit in the subjects which
they undertook." Probably Wordsworth took the Classical subject—
3, 10, 15 *Sat.*, Juvenal.

Men did not take an examination in the Michaelmas term of
their fourth year nor were they required to give in themes. In that
term and in the preceding Long Vacation those who wished to do
well in the University examinations were working strenuously for
these. Wordsworth had abandoned that idea and spent the Long
Vacation on the continent, not returning to Cambridge until late in
the term. The reports confirm his own account of his reading in
The Prelude and in his letters. He could distinguish himself in work
in which he was interested but did not attempt to excel in the general
curriculum. "I did not", he wrote to Miss Taylor in 1801, "as I in
some respects greatly regret, devote myself to the studies of the
University." (*Early Letters*, ed. de Selincourt, no. 120.)

Wordsworth's Cambridge Friends and Schoolfellows

On his arrival in Cambridge Wordsworth was greeted by his school friends:

> Some Friends I had, acquaintances who there
> Seem'd Friends, poor simple schoolboys, now hung round
> With honour and importance.*

Some of these were doubtless schoolfellows from Hawkshead—senior men, for they were "hung round with honour and importance". Among them was Charles Farish, who went up to Trinity as a sizar in 1784 and migrated to Queens'. He was fifteenth wrangler in 1788, became a Fellow of his College and entered the Church. In a note to an early poem Wordsworth refers to a line as "from a short MS. poem read to me when an undergraduate, by my schoolfellow and friend, Charles Farish....The verses were by a brother of his...'.†
At St John's was John Fleming of Rayrigg, son of the Rev. William Raincock of Cumberland, the boy with whom he used to walk round the lake at Esthwaite in the morning before school hours, "repeating favourite verses with one voice",‡ who had come up in 1785. Fleming was his father's eldest son and changed his name on succeeding to an uncle's estates. He was fifth wrangler in 1789, took Orders and became Rector of Bootle in Cumberland. Of their early friendship Wordsworth wrote in 1805, "we live as if those hours had never been".§ Of the Hawkshead boys who came up in 1786, William Penny was at St John's. He entered as a pensioner on Frewen's side, became a scholar and was later ordained. Edward Joseph Birkett was at Christ's. He graduated in 1790; he may have been the occupant of Milton's rooms on whom Wordsworth called on a memorable occasion.‖ William Raincock, Fleming's brother, of Pembroke, was second wrangler in 1790 and became a Fellow of his College. In the art of making a musical instrument of his fingers, Wordsworth said that "William Raincock of Rayrigg, a fine-spirited lad, took the lead of all my schoolfellows".¶

Of his own year from Hawkshead were Thomas Holden Gawthrop of St John's and Robert Hodgson Greenwood of Trinity. According to custom at the school, boys who were leaving made a present of books to the School library. Greenwood, Wordsworth, John Miller and Gawthrop joined to present Gillies's *History of Greece* and Hoole's *Tasso's Jerusalem.*** Gawthrop was Lupton Fellow at St John's

---

* *Prelude* (1805), II, ll. 17–19.
† A. B. Grosart, *The Prose Works of William Wordsworth*, III, p. 11.
‡ *Memoirs of William Wordsworth*, I, 40.   § *Prelude*, II, ll. 358.
‖ *Prelude*, III, ll. 295, "my class-fellow at School".
¶ *Prelude* (ed. de Selincourt), Notes, p. 531.
** See *The Eagle*, no. 105, for an article on the Library at Hawkshead Grammar School by Canon A. Earle.

(though his name does not appear in the Tripos lists) and became in due course a Senior Fellow and Steward of the College. In 1815 the College presented him to the living of Marston Morteyne. Greenwood, at school, was "the minstrel of our troop" in the boating excursions on Windermere, who "blew his flute alone upon the rock".* He was admitted a sizar at Trinity, was sixteenth wrangler and was elected a Fellow of the College in 1792. His disposition was perhaps not much changed. Wordsworth writes of him to Matthews (August 1791), "He seems to me to have much of Yorick in his disposition; at least Yorick, if I am not mistaken, had a deal of the male mad-cap in him, but G. out mad-caps him quite".† In March 1835 Wordsworth was staying with his brother at Trinity Lodge and writing to Robert Jones mentions "Greenwood, my old schoolfellow—he is still here residing as Senior Fellow—he looks pretty well, but complains of many infirmities".‡

Junior to Wordsworth from his old school were Thomas Holme Maude and Thomas Jack who came up to St John's in 1788. Maude was a junior optime in 1792, but became Ashton Fellow of the College in 1795 and was afterwards a banker in Kendal. Jack was fourth wrangler in 1792 and Simpson Fellow in 1804. He succeeded Wordsworth's uncle as rector at Forncett. Other Hawkshead boys of that year were Rudd of Trinity, tenth wrangler, and later a Fellow of his College, and Balderston (St Catharine's) and Chambre (Peterhouse), junior optimes; of 1789 were Thomas Harrison of Queens', senior wrangler in 1793, and Sykes of Sidney Sussex, tenth wrangler; of 1790, Thomas Younge of Trinity, twelfth wrangler. All three became Fellows of their Colleges. Harrison went to the Bar and was a keen supporter of the anti-Slave Trade movement. Younge became a tutor of Trinity.

The Hawkshead boys were an able lot. They came up well prepared for their University work and many of them did well. For a Hawkshead boy of his ability, Wordsworth's Cambridge career was an exceptional one.

Of his schoolfellows, Fleming and Raincock seem to have been his closest friends, though some of the others are referred to in his correspondence. Other friendships were made at Cambridge, both at St John's and other colleges. Writing to Montagu in 1844, he says: "My intimate associates of my own College are all gone long since. Myers, my cousin, Terrot, Jones, my fellow-traveller, Fleming and his brother, Raincock of Pembroke, Bishop Middleton of the same College—it has pleased God that I should survive them all."§

---

* *Prelude*, II, ll. 174–6. *Memoirs*, I, 41.
† *The Early Letters of William and Dorothy Wordsworth* (ed. de Selincourt), no. 15.   ‡ *Letters* (ed. de Selincourt), no. 1106.
§ *Letters* (ed. de Selincourt), no. 1546.

Of John Myers, the son of his father's sister Ann, who came up from Sedbergh and was admitted a sizar under Frewen, we have already spoken.

William Terrot of Berwick-on-Tweed, to whom he always refers affectionately, was the son of Captain Charles Terrot of the Invalids, of French descent. Terrot came out in the senior optimes in the Mathematical Tripos of 1791, was ordained and became a chaplain in the Royal Navy and was for some time Master of the Greenwich Hospital School.

Robert Jones, though he did not take an Honours degree, was elected in 1791 to one of the Welsh Fellowships at St John's. He was ordained and was later presented by the College to the living of Souldern in Oxfordshire. To him Wordsworth dedicated his *Descriptive Sketches* in 1793. Jones looked back on their famous journey as "the golden and sunny spot in his life", so Dorothy wrote to Mrs Clarkson in 1831: "It would delight you to hear the pair talk of their adventures. My Brother, active, lively and almost as strong as ever on a mountain top; Jones, fat and roundabout and rosy, and puffing and panting while he climbs the little hill from the road to our house."*

Thomas Fanshaw Middleton, of Pembroke, was from Christ's Hospital, a Grecian and schoolfellow of Coleridge and Lamb. He graduated senior optime in 1792, was ordained, and in 1814 became the first Bishop of Calcutta.

Two other Cambridge men who were his contemporaries and became lifelong friends of his were Basil Montagu of Christ's College, sixth wrangler in 1790, and Francis Wrangham of Magdalene and Trinity Hall, third wrangler in 1790 and First Chancellor's medallist. They shared his revolutionary views, but like him moderated their opinions with advancing years. It is possible that they may have met in their undergraduate days. In writing to Wrangham in 1835† Wordsworth refers to the death of "Rudd of Trinity, Fleming just gone", as if both had known them. But the men with whom he was in touch and correspondence in the years immediately after he went down were Matthews, Jones, Terrot, Myers and Raincock. Matthews went to the West Indies about 1800 to practise law and died there; Myers died in 1821, Terrot in 1832, Robert Jones in 1835.

[NOTE. Most of the particulars about the Johnians in this Note are taken from Sir Robert Scott's brief biographies in his *Admissions*, Part IV. Other sources are the *Historical Register* and *Alumni Cantabrigienses*.]

* *Letters* (ed. de Selincourt), no. 982.
† Ibid. no. 1099.

The Admonition Book

The Admonition Book records offences against College rules and the penalties inflicted, but the record ends just before Wordsworth's time. In Dr Powell's active decade, thirty-three men were formally admonished for one offence or another. Chevallier recorded only one case and with that the book ends. The last entries are as follows:

Nov. 25, 1780. I, William Cosens, was admonished by the Master before the Seniors, for going out of College while I had an Aegrotat, and refusing to do the punishment set me by my Tutor.

Witness J. C.

Decʳ. 13, 1780. I, William Cosens, was admonished by the Master before the Seniors, for not complying with the Punishment imposed upon me by the Master and Seniors.   J. C.

It is unlikely that breaches of discipline ceased in 1780, indeed Wordsworth himself makes clear that they were sometimes flagrant. What probably happened was that the Master, Chevallier, whose health was failing, ceased to deal with these matters, and as the Master kept the book, no record of them was made and the Admonition Book fell into disuse.

The Seniority

The senior Fellows in 1787 included Sir Isaac Pennington, at the time Professor of Chemistry, and later Regius Professor of Physic; Thomas Gisborne, who became President of the College of Physicians in 1791 and Physician in Ordinary to the King; William Craven, Professor of Arabic, who succeeded Chevallier as Master; John Mainwaring, Lady Margaret Professor in 1788; and William Pearce, the Senior Tutor and Public Orator, who was elected Master of Jesus in 1789 and was twice Vice-Chancellor.

Admissions in the years 1785–1790

	1784–5	1785–6	1786–7	1787–8	1788–9	1789–90	Totals
Noblemen	1	2	—	1	2	—	6
Fellow Commoners	5	4	10	4	9	6	38
Pensioners	29	29	31	32	32	27	180
Sizars	15	12	15	7	8	10	67
*Oxonians	4	1	2	—	—	1	8
M.A. of Gonville and Caius	—	—	—	—	—	1	1
Totals	54	48	58	44	51	45	300

* "It will be observed that a fair number of Bachelors of Arts of Oxford were admitted to the College and graduated as Masters of Arts of Cambridge. Their object was to qualify for holding benefices in plurality by dispensation". (Sir R. F. Scott, *Admissions*, IV, preface, p. ix.)

E. A. B.

WORDSWORTH'S ASH TREE

The Prelude, Book VI, ll. 66–94.

WHERE in "our Groves and tributary walks"* was Wordsworth's ash tree? *The Prelude* does not record its position. Nor does Dorothy Wordsworth, who saw the tree when she visited Cambridge some nineteen years after her brother had gone down from St John's. In a letter to Lady Beaumont, dated 14 August in the year 1810, she wrote: "We walked in the groves all the morning, and visited the Colleges. I sought out a favourite ash-tree, which my brother speaks of in his poem on his own life—a tree covered with ivy".† On the same day she wrote to William himself and to Sara Hutchinson: "I was charmed with the walks, found out William's ashtree; the fine willow is dying...".‡

Ash trees are not characteristic of the Backs,§ and there is no reason to suppose that they were ever numerous in the College grounds. The characteristic trees in the grounds of St John's since the seventeenth century have been elms, and they were perhaps at their finest when Wordsworth was an undergraduate—

Lofty Elms,
Inviting shades of opportune recess,
Did give composure to a neighbourhood
Unpeaceful in itself.

They grew beside St John's Ditch (where the New Court now stands), along the Broad Walk, and round the meadow‖—an arrangement already shown in David Loggan's view and plan of 1688. Some of the elms that Wordsworth knew had certainly been planted in the seventeenth century,¶ and two of those ancient trees survived until the great storm of 14 October 1881, when the last of the "Seven Sisters", which grew in the meadow, to the east of the Fellows'

---

* Quotations from *The Prelude* are from the text of 1805.

† *The Letters of William and Dorothy Wordsworth: the Middle Years*, arranged and edited by Ernest de Selincourt, 1937, vol. I, 1806–June 1811, p. 388.

‡ Ibid. p. 392.

§ It is, however, interesting to note that seventy-two ash trees were planted in the grounds of Queens' College in 1630 (Willis and Clark, *Architectural History*, vol. II, p. 57).

‖ Cf. G. Dyer, *History of the University and Colleges of Cambridge*, 1814, vol. II, p. 266: "...so, passing over yon elegant stone bridge, you may be pleased, in ranging down those winding walks, which so agreeably skirt the Cam, or those straight walks, adorned with lofty elms, conducting to the Fellows' garden."

¶ Willis and Clark, *Architectural History*, vol. II, pp. 322f.

Garden, were blown down.* No doubt some of the elms beside
St John's Ditch and along the Broad Walk that were cut down when
the New Court was built dated from the same period.

Wordsworth's ash tree, in contrast with the lines of elms, was
"a single tree"—

> A single Tree
> There was, no doubt yet standing there, an Ash
> With sinuous trunk, boughs exquisitely wreath'd;
> Up from the ground and almost to the top
> The trunk and master branches everywhere
> Were green with ivy.

Any record of an ash in the grounds at that date is therefore of
interest. By chance, there is evidence of an ash tree in the grounds
of St John's in 1805, fourteen years after William left Cambridge
and five years before Dorothy's visit, and its position can be located
within narrow limits.

The Inclosure Award for the parish of St Giles, dated 14 May
1805, contains a precise description of the parish boundary. The
boundary runs up the centre of the Bin Brook from a point near the
south-west corner of the present Benson Court of Magdalene College
as far as the point where the brook is joined by the ditch that forms
the eastern boundary of the Fellows' Garden, some twenty-five yards
to the north of the present iron bridge. At the latter point the
boundary leaves the brook and runs south, crossing the walk just to
the west of the iron bridge, enters the Fellows' Garden near the
present iron gate, continues in a straight line through the eastern part
of the Garden, and then runs up the ditch that forms the western
boundary of Trinity College meadow. It should be noted that in
Wordsworth's time the Bin Brook, which to-day is carried through
a culvert from the north-west corner of the Fellows' Garden, under
the walk, and as far as the point, north of the iron bridge, where it
is joined by the ditch that bounds the Garden on the east, was an
open stream and formed the northern boundary of this part of the
College property. The present College orchard, north of the walk
that leads to Queen's Road, still belonged to Merton College,
Oxford, from which it was obtained by exchange under the Inclosure
Award in 1805. The end of the present culvert marks the junction of
the brook and the ditch referred to above, and thus the point at
which the parish boundary leaves the brook and runs southwards

---

* J. W. Clark, "Our Old Trees" in *The Cambridge Review*, no. 52
(26 October 1881); T. McKenny Hughes in *Cambridge Antiquarian Society
Proceedings*, vol. v, 1880–4, pp. xxxix–xli; "Our College Grounds" in *The
Eagle*, no. LXVI (January 1882), pp. 46–51. A section of the trunk of one of
these last survivors of the "Seven Sisters" is preserved in the museum of
the Botany School.

across the walk. It should also be noted that, until the New Court was begun in 1827, the Bin Brook and the river were connected by a ditch, called St John's Ditch, which formed the southern boundary of the Pond Yard or Fishponds Close. This ditch left the brook at a point west of the New Court, approximately opposite the present northern boundary of the orchard, ran across the site now occupied by the New Court, and joined the river a little to the north of the present New Court bridge. The Inclosure Award, in tracing the parish boundary, mentions three boundary marks in the College grounds. One of these was "an Ash Tree marked with a Cross in Saint John's College Walks by the side of the said Brook",* viz. the Bin Brook. It is clear from the context that this ash tree grew by the brook either at some point between the junction of the brook with St John's Ditch and its junction with the ditch that forms the eastern boundary of the Fellows' Garden (a distance of not more than fifty yards) or just to the north of the present iron bridge in the sharp angle then formed by the open brook and the latter ditch. The latter position is perhaps probable, since the tree would then have indicated the point at which the parish boundary leaves the brook to run southwards across the walk, and this would account for the cross, or boundary mark, cut in its trunk. It was in any case on the right bank of the brook, since it was in St John's College walks.

The area of the present College orchard, north of the walk leading to Queen's Road, is described in the Award as at that time "part of a Garden or Orchard belonging to the Warden and Scholars of Merton College" and, as such, probably did not contain many trees of great height. Thus, as seen from the College walks, the ash tree may have stood clear against the western sky; and, as carrying a boundary mark, it was probably a well-established tree of some size.

It cannot, of course, be proved that this was the ash of which Wordsworth wrote

> Oft have I stood
> Foot-bound, uplooking at this lovely Tree
> Beneath a frosty moon.

Yet may it not be that the three Commissioners† appointed under the Act of 42 George III for the Inclosure of the Parish of St Giles,

* The description of the boundary, so far as it relates to the College grounds, is quoted in full in *The Eagle*, no. 235 (August 1949), p. 155, where the relevant portion of the Plan of the Parish of St Giles (dated 1804) made on the Inclosure is also reproduced (p. 149).

† One of the Commissioners was William Custance, of Cambridge, surveyor and builder, author of *A New Plan of the University and Town of Cambridge to the Present Year, 1798*, the map which best represents the Cambridge that Wordsworth knew.

by their meticulous description of their perambulation of the parish
boundary, unwittingly provided the only enduring record of the spot
at which his ash tree grew?

It is interesting to notice that ash trees still grow in the same region.
One grows on the left bank of the Bin Brook a little to the south of
the northern boundary of the orchard; another at a point in the
orchard which was on the left bank of the brook when the brook was
an open stream. A third, the largest of the three, grew between these
two, also on what was formerly the brook's left bank. This third tree
died in the summer of 1949 and was cut down in March 1950. Its
rings showed it to have been about 165 years old. Wordsworth may
therefore have known it as a small sapling. These three trees may
have been planted deliberately along the brook. Yet is it not also just
possible that they struck root there by chance, from seeds

> That hung in yellow tassels and festoons

upon a tree now vanished but immortal?   J. S. B. S.

CORRIGENDA

In the catalogue (*opposite*) references to the pagination
of the plates refer only to *The Eagle*, vol. LIV, no. 237,
from which this book is reprinted, and should be ignored.

The numbers of the plates have not been changed,
and these will provide the necessary cross-references.

WORDSWORTH PORTRAITS:
A BIOGRAPHICAL CATALOGUE*

1 *Painting by* WILLIAM SHUTER, 1798.

Dorothy Wordsworth wrote in her Alfoxden journal for 6 May 1798: "Expected the painter and Coleridge." Soon after, Coleridge, writing to Joseph Cottle about the printing of *Lyrical Ballads*, remarked: "The picture shall be sent." When Cottle published the letter, he added a footnote to Coleridge's bare statement: "A portrait of Mr Wordsworth, correctly and beautifully executed, by an artist then at Stowey; now in my possession." The artist's conception of Wordsworth agrees marvellously with Hazlitt's description of him when he visited Alfoxden in 1798:

There is a severe, worn presence of thought about the temples, a fire in his eye (as if he saw something in objects more than outward appearance), an intense, high, narrow forehead, a Roman nose, cheeks furrowed by strong purpose and feeling, and a convulsive inclination to laughter about the mouth, a good deal at variance with the solemn, stately expression of the rest of his face.

Professor de Selincourt considered this the earliest known portrait, but it could not have been taken more than a few months before Hancock's (No. 2), because the subject left for Germany in September 1798. William Shuter exhibited paintings at the Royal Academy from 1771 to 1791. At that time his speciality was fruit.

Three-quarter face turned to the left, half-length, left hand thrust into waistcoat (characteristic). The original is in Cornell University Library. There is a photogravure of it by Hanfstaengl in St John's College Library, and an engraving of it appears in de Selincourt's edition of the journals of Dorothy Wordsworth. (*Journals of Dorothy Wordsworth*, ed. de Selincourt, 1941, p. 16 and n.; Joseph Cottle, *Reminiscences of Samuel Taylor Coleridge ~nd Robert Southey*, 1847, p. 180; P. P. Howe, *William Hazlitt*, Penguin, 1948, p. 65; Graves, *Dictionary of Artists...*, 1901, article on Shuter; Broughton, *The Wordsworth Collection...given to Cornell University...: a Catalogue*, 1931, p. 112.)

2 *Pencil and chalk drawing by* ROBERT HANCOCK, 1798.

Executed for Joseph Cottle, who also commissioned the Hancock portraits of Coleridge, Southey and Lamb. Of this portrait he said: "An undoubted likeness, universally acknowledged to be so at the time." In 1836, Crabb Robinson visited Cottle at Bristol, saw the pictures, noted in his diary that "Wordsworth resembles E. Lytton Bulwer more than himself now", and wrote to Wordsworth: "You have taken abundant care to let the world know that you did not

* The author and the editors gratefully acknowledge the assistance of Miss Helen Darbishire in the preparation of this article.

marry Mrs W: for her beauty. Now this picture will justify the inference that she too had a higher motive for her acceptance of you...." When the good Mrs W. wrote to Robinson during that same year, she recalled a time "7 or 8 years ago" when the family "were favoured with a sight of the Portraits—to the best of *my* recollection we were most pleased with that of Southey....Dora said that of her Father's reminded her of her Brother John." In his life of Wordsworth Professor Harper gave the date of this portrait as "about 1796", and the article on Hancock in *D.N.B.* dates the whole group "about 1796". In Cottle's *Reminiscences*, however, there are engravings of each of the four with the dates underneath; Wordsworth and Lamb are dated 1798; Coleridge and Southey, 1796. Hancock was a Bristol artist.

See plate facing p. 113. The original, with the flesh tinted by red crayon is in the National Portrait Gallery. (Joseph Cottle, *Early Recollections chiefly relating to Samuel Taylor Coleridge*, 1837, pp. xxxii, 250; *Correspondence of Crabb Robinson with the Wordsworth Circle*, ed. Morley, 1927, pp. 316, 323; Basil Long, *British Miniaturists working between 1520 and 1860*, 1924; *Wordsworth's Poetical Works*, ed. Knight, 1889, vol. x, pp. 403-4; *Catalogue of the National Portrait Gallery*, 1950.)

3   *Painting by* WILLIAM HAZLITT, 1803.

Hazlitt intended this painting for Sir George Beaumont. Coleridge wrote to Southey on 1 August 1803, "Young Hazlitt has taken masterly portraits of me and Wordsworth", and two days later he wrote Wordsworth:

Mrs Wilkinson *swears* that your portrait is 20 years too old for you—and mine equally too old, and too lank—every single person without one exception cries out! What a likeness! but the face is too long! You have a round face! Hazlitt knows this; but he will not alter it. Why? because the likeness with him is a secondary consideration— he wants it to be a fine Picture. Hartley knew yours instantly—and Derwent too, but Hartley said—it is very like; but Wordsworth is far handsomer....The true defects of it as a likeness are that the eyes are *too open and full*—and there is a heaviness given to the forehead from the parting the Hair so greasily and pomatumish—there should have been a few straggling hairs left.

Writing to Tom Wedgewood on 16 September, Coleridge praised Hazlitt as a "thinking, observant, original man, of great power as a Painter of Character Portraits, and far more in the manner of the old Painters, than any living artist, but the objects must be *before* him; he has no imaginative memory". A few weeks later he wrote to Sir George Beaumont, and referred to the pictures in passing: "We have not heard of or from Hazlitt. He is at Manchester, we suppose, and has both portraits with him." Southey passed on the news of the portraits to his artist friend, Richard Duppa, in a letter of 6 December: "[Hazlitt] has made a very fine picture of Coleridge for Sir George Beaumont...; he has also painted Wordsworth, but so dismally...that one of his friends, on seeing it, exclaimed 'At the gallows—deeply affected by his deserved fate—yet determined to die like a man.'" Thirty years later, in a letter to Hazlitt's son, Wordsworth recollected seeing Hazlitt in "the year 1803 or 1804, when he passed some time in this neighbourhood. He was then practising portrait-painting with professional views. At his desire I sat to him, but as he did not satisfy himself or my friends, the unfinished work was destroyed." If one of the two portraits Hazlitt had with him at Manchester was his portrait of Wordsworth, it is quite possible that the ageing poet's memory erred, and that the portrait remains somewhere intact but unrecognized.

(*Unpublished Letters of Samuel Taylor Coleridge*, ed. Griggs, 1932, vol. I, pp. 265 and n., 267–8; Knight, *Memorials of Coleorton*, 1887, vol. I, pp. 24–5; *Life and Correspondence of Robert Southey*, ed. C. C. Southey, 1850, vol. II, p. 238; P. P. Howe, *Life of William Hazlitt*, Penguin, 1949, pp. 93 and n., 430.)

4 *Carnation-tinted pencil drawing by* HENRY EDRIDGE, 1805.

In 1804 Edridge made his first acquaintance with the Wordsworths. "We have seen a Mr Edridge who talked with us about you—he seems a very pleasing man...", Dorothy wrote to Lady Beaumont in October of that year. Edridge also impressed her brother as "a man of very mild and pleasing manners, and as far as I could judge, of delicate feelings, in the province of his Art". This statement is part of a letter written to Sir George Beaumont on Christmas Day of 1804, but it makes no mention of a portrait. Edridge must have completed it by March 1805 when Sir George wrote to Wordsworth: "I admire him both as a man and an artist, and wish he had drawn all your portraits when he was at Grasmere." When Edridge was taking his likeness, the poet was hard at work finishing *The Prelude*. Professor de Selincourt called it "the only known portrait of the poet in his prime", and it appears in several of his editions of Wordsworth. Edridge was a miniature painter, a good friend of the Beaumonts, who became an Associate of the Royal Academy in 1820.

Three-quarter face turned to the left, quarter-length. In the lower left-hand corner is written almost illegibly "H.E.: 18[05?]". The drawing is used as the frontispiece of de Selincourt's edition of *The Prelude*. The original is in the possession of Mrs Rawnsley, Allan Bank, Grasmere. (*Prelude*, ed. de Selincourt, 1926, p. viii and n.; *Letters of William and Dorothy Wordsworth: Early Years*, ed. de Selincourt, 1935, pp. 418 and n., 424.)

5 *Life mask by* BENJAMIN HAYDON, 1815.

Haydon was a painter of grand historical subjects who was never contented to attempt anything less than a masterpiece. He usually took four or five years to complete a canvas. In order to secure models which could be studied at length he used to make sketches and take casts of whatever he thought might be of value, whether it was a figure from the Elgin Marbles, or the body of a negro he saw passing in the street. When Wordsworth made one of his occasional visits to London in April 1815, Haydon must have seized the opportunity of adding the poet's face to his collection. "I had a cast made yesterday of Wordsworth's face", he writes in his journal for 15 April. "He bore it like a philosopher." Haydon's paintings caused a sensation in his own time, but he is now known chiefly for his passionate defence of the worth and antiquity of the. Elgin Marbles, his fascinating autobiography, and his dependence on the generosity of his friends, notably Keats, to help him meet the enormous expenses of "High Art", as he always called it. When Haydon's vogue ran out along with the patience of his creditors he tried to make a living by portraiture, but he painted too honestly for that. He shot himself in 1846.

The manner in which one of the several known casts of Haydon's mask came into the possession of St John's College is recorded in Council Minute 1022/7, dated 19 April 1918:

Gift to the College

The Master reported that Mrs Butler had offered to the College a death mask of Wordsworth found among the effects of the late Master of Trinity [H. M. Butler, *ob.* 1918], and that he had provisionally accepted it. It was agreed to approve the action of the Master and to ask him to convey the thanks of the College to Mrs Butler.

Correspondence between Mr Previté Orton, then Librarian of St John's, and the National Portrait Gallery established that Mrs Butler's gift to the College was a cast from the same mould as the Gallery's cast of Haydon's *life* mask of 1815. Presumably the cast was left in Trinity Master's Lodge by the poet's brother Christopher, who was Master of that College from 1820 to 1841.

See a hitherto unpublished photograph of the cast now in St John's Library, the frontispiece. A photograph of the cast in the National Portrait Gallery appears as the frontispiece to Herbert Read's *Wordsworth*. There is a cast in the Ashmolean Museum, and another in the Wordsworth Museum, Grasmere. (*Life of B. R. Haydon*, ed. Tom Taylor, 1853, vol. 1, p. 297; *Catalogue of the National Portrait Gallery*, 1949; *Catalogue of Oxford Portraits*, 1912, p. 206; *Catalogue of Dove Cottage*, 1947, p. 33.)

6 *Paper profile by* S I R G E O R G E B E A U M O N T, 1815.

Executed for Benjamin Haydon. The relationship between Wordsworth and Haydon seems to have grown during this year to one of
mutual respect and admiration, and Haydon became increasingly
enamoured with the idea of painting a masterpiece in which the
poet Wordsworth would figure as a subject. Evidently he found he
needed more to work from than half of the head in plaster, and
desired to have a bust made. In order to accomplish this project
he asked Wordsworth to supply him with supplementary facts about
the shape of his head. Wordsworth answered (12 September 1815):

Agreeable to your request, (for which I am much obliged to you,
and to your friend for his offer of undertaking the Bust) I forwarded
to you from Rydale Mount a few days ago the dimensions of my
pericranium, taken by the hand of Sir George Beaumont—He is
entitled to our common thanks for he exerted not a little upon the
occasion; and I hope the performance will answer your purpose.
Sir George begged me say that the hair on that part of the skull where
the crown is, is thin; so that a little of the skull appears bald; and
Sir George thinks that a similar baldness might have a good effect in
the bust. I should have sent the drawing immediately on Receipt of
your Letter, but I had nobody near who could execute it.

It is reasonable to suppose that some of the pericranial statistics
Haydon wanted were given by Sir George's profile, which was life-
size. Haydon wrote on the bottom of it: "Wordsworth, a profile
sketched and cut out by Sir George Beaumont, when I was going
to have a bust of him." Haydon, I take it, does not mean that he
went anywhere to model a bust, but that he once *intended* to take
one, or have it taken. No such bust is known to have existed, and
probably it never was made. Haydon, nevertheless, was pleased to
have Sir George's work, and Wordsworth wrote to assure him that
Sir George and Lady B., his wife and his sister thought it resembled
him much, "but Mrs W. is sure that the upper part of the forehead
does not project as much as mine".

About this time Wordsworth began to look upon Haydon as
a kindred spirit, a fellow practitioner of "High Art". Haydon, for
his part, was writing in his journal: "He is a great being and will
hereafter be ranked as one who had a portion of the spirit of the
mighty ones...." And in December 1815 Wordsworth was inspired
to address a sonnet to Haydon, beginning

> High is our calling, Friend! Creative Art,
> (Whether the instrument of words she use
> Or pencil pregnant with ethereal hues),
> Demands the service of a mind and heart
> ...heroically fashioned.

When he received the letter containing this and two other sonnets, Haydon said characteristically: "Up I went into the clouds."

Sir George Beaumont was a patron of poets and painters who dabbled in both arts himself. He was one of the four founders of the National Gallery.

In 1889 the profile was in the possession of a Mr Stephen Pearce, Cavendish Square, who bought it at a sale of Haydon's effects in 1852. (*Wordsworth's Poetical Works*, ed. Knight, 1889, vol. x, p. 428; *Life of Haydon*, ed. Tom Taylor, 1853, vol. 1, pp. 297, 325; *Letters of William and Dorothy Wordsworth: Middle Years*, ed. de Selincourt, 1937, pp. 679–80, 681; *D.N.B.* article on Sir George Beaumont.)

7 *Portrait of Wordsworth in "Christ's Entry into Jerusalem" by* BENJAMIN HAYDON, 1817.

After toiling for six years over this painting, Haydon finished it in 1820, but it is evident that Wordsworth was painted in as an onlooker at *Christ's Entry* some time before the end of 1817. Wordsworth took a great interest in the progress of the work long before he became so intimately connected with it, as his letters to Haydon testify. "I hope Christ's entry into Jerusalem goes on to your satisfaction", he wrote in September 1815: "I cannot doubt but that Picture will do you huge credit; and raise the Reputation of Art in this Country." Early in 1816 the poet wrote the painter a long letter of advice on how best to interpret the scene. In the same year or early in 1817 Haydon had a brainstorm: "I now put Hazlitt's head into my picture, looking at Christ as an investigator. It had a good effect. I then put Keats in the background, and resolved to introduce Wordsworth bowing in reverence and awe. Wordsworth was highly pleased, and before the close of the season (1817), the picture was three parts done." Besides Hazlitt the investigator, and Wordsworth the worshipper, Haydon had put in Voltaire as a sneerer and Newton as a believer. Hearing of this in January 1817 Wordsworth wrote: "I am sensible of the honour done me by placing my head in such company and heartily congratulate you on the progress which you have made in your picture...."

Wordsworth's bowing head was based on a black chalk drawing on tinted paper which may have been taken as early as 1816; the date depends on whether Wordsworth's letter acknowledges the fact of his image on the canvas, or merely Haydon's intention of putting it there. It is not known how Haydon arranged a sitting for the sketch, there being no record of Wordsworth's presence in London from April 1815 until December 1817, when his presence in the painting was certainly a fact. Haydon may have come to Rydal on an excursion from London he made in 1816, though neither he nor Wordsworth has left a record of such a visit. Haydon marked the sketch "Wordsworth. For entry into Jerusalem, 1819", but this date must apply to his completion of the whole painting. The sketch was sold at an auction of Haydon's effects in 1852.

Wordsworth's letter of 7 April 1817 shows him a willing collaborator in Haydon's grand undertaking: "I have had a cast taken of one of my hands, with which, I hope, Southey will charge himself [to bring to London]—You expressed a wish for an opportunity to paint them from the life—I hope this substitute may not be wholly useless to you." In December Keats and Wordsworth met for the first time at a dinner given by Haydon, and the painter was overjoyed at his having arranged the historic event:

It was indeed an immortal evening. Wordsworth's fine intonation... Keats's eager inspired look, Lamb's quaint sparkle of lambent humour....It was a night worthy of the Elizabethan age, and my solemn Jerusalem flashing up by the flame of the fire, with Christ hanging over us like a vision, all made up a picture which will long glow upon "...that inward eye / Which is the bliss of solitude".

When the work was finished in 1820, Wordsworth thought that if he could see it, "it would inspire me with a sonnet". Haydon wanted to hire a hall, to hang it in style, but was sunk too low in debt. In desperation he approached his friends for loans, including Wordsworth. That somewhat cooled the poet's ardour: "It is some time since I have been impelled to lay down a rule, not to lend to *a Friend* any money which I cannot afford *to lose*....I hope your Picture is not much hurt by my Presence in it, though heaven knows I feel I have little right to be there." The picture finally was exhibited, however. Mrs Siddons pronounced the Christ "absolutely successful", and Haydon made £1300 from admissions and the sale of leaflets. Still Crabb Robinson was not impressed: "The group of Wordsworth, Newton, and Voltaire is ill-executed. The poet is a forlorn and haggard old man; the philosopher is a sleek, well-dressed citizen of London; and Voltaire is merely an ugly Frenchman."

Wordsworth stands on the right side of the picture, half-length, three-quarter turned to the left, head bowed, hand on breast. Above him is Keats, and behind him are Voltaire and Newton. The painting is now in the Cincinnati, Ohio, Art Museum. A detail photograph showing the group described above appears in Harper, *Wordsworth*, 1929. The sketch for this picture was a head, larger than life, three-quarter turned to the left, bowed. It was in the possession of Mr Stephen Pearce, Cavendish Square, in 1889. (*Life of Haydon*, ed. Tom Taylor, 1853, vol. I, pp. 239, 371–2, 387, 404 and 410; *Letters of William and Dorothy Wordsworth: Middle Years*, ed. de Selincourt, 1937, pp. 680, 781, 861, 862; ibid. *Later Years*, 1939, p. 1367; *Wordsworth's Poetical Works*, ed. Knight, 1889, vol. x, pp. 407–8.)

8 *Painting by* RICHARD CARRUTHERS, 1817.

The artist wrote Thomas Monkhouse that he took a sketch for a portrait in oils at Rydal in the summer of 1817, and completed the painting in November of that year. When Dorothy Wordsworth remarked, "William has sate for his picture", in a letter from Rydal dated 16 October 1817, she must have been referring to Carruthers's painting. She thought it a "charming" picture. Wordsworth characterized the artist in a letter to Francis Chantrey three years later: "I have requested Mr Carruthers who painted a Portrait of me some years ago, to call for a sight of the Bust [No. 11]—He is an amiable young Man whom a favourable opening induced to sacrifice the Pencil for the Pen...of the Counting House which he is successfully driving at Lisbon."

Three-quarter face turned to the left, left hand in waistcoat pocket (characteristic), seated against a tree, background of mountain tops and a fast mountain stream. Now owned by Miss Hutchinson of Grantsfield, Kimbolton, Leominster. Carruthers made a copy which belonged to Mrs Drew, daughter of Thomas Monkhouse, in 1889. (*Wordsworth's Poetical Works*, ed. Knight, 1889, vol. x, pp. 405–6; *Letters of William and Dorothy Wordsworth: Middle Years*, ed. de Selincourt, 1937, pp. 801–2; *Correspondence of Crabb Robinson with the Wordsworth Circle*, ed. Morley, 1927, p. 104.)

9 *Pencil and chalk drawing on tinted paper by* BENJAMIN HAYDON, 1818.

Haydon presented this drawing to Wordsworth. The inscription at the foot is still for the most part legible and it reads: "B R Haydon / in respect & affection / 17th Jany 18??" The poet has signed it: "Wm Wordsworth/aetat 48 1818." Wordsworth must have been referring to this sketch (there was no other taken during that period) in his letter to Haydon of 16 January 1820: "Your most valuable Drawing arrived, when I was unable to enjoy it as it deserved.... Your drawing is much admired as a work of art; some think it a stodgy likeness; but in general it is not deemed so—for my own part I am proud to possess it as a mark of your regard and for its own merits...." Perhaps Haydon used the sketch for touching up his *Christ's Entry*, and presented it to Wordsworth during his financial crisis of 1820. A few weeks after thanking Haydon for the sketch, Wordsworth was putting off his advances for a loan.

The artist has been accused of giving his subject too large a development at the back of the head. This may be so, but his head was enormous, and it had a great bump at the back of it; the poet has recorded his occasional difficulty in finding a hat large enough to fit him. But there seems to have been too much of Haydon in the drawing for the sensibilities of the Wordsworth family. Dorothy thought "the sketch by Haydon is a fine drawing, but what a like-ness! All that there is of likeness makes it to me the more disagree-able." It has been said that William called it "the brigand".

See reproduction facing p. 120. Head and shoulders, three-quarter turned to the left. The original is now in the National Portrait Gallery. There is an autotype of it in St John's Library. A reproduction of it appears in D. Wellesley, *English Poets in Pictures: Wordsworth.* (*Letters of William and Dorothy Words-worth: Middle Years*, ed. de Selincourt, 1937, pp. 860, 861–2; ibid. *Later Years*, p. 557; *Wordsworth's Poetical Works*, ed. Knight, 1889, vol. x, pp. 409–10; *London Times Literary Supplement*, 28 April 1950, p. 261.)

10 *Pencil drawing by* EDWARD NASH, 1818.

Executed for Southey. This is the handsomest likeness in exist-ence, and it catches an irresistibly pleasant whimsical expression. Wordsworth suffered much in later life from an eye affliction, which made reading and writing very difficult for him. In preparing her book, *The Later Wordsworth*, Miss E. C. Batho consulted an ophthalmologist on the subject, giving him several portraits as evidence. The Nash and Carruthers (No. 8) drawings in particular suggested the disease trachoma, brought to England by troops who had been stationed in Egypt and the West Indies. Nash was a friend and protégé of Southey's who painted several portraits for the Southey family.

Head three-quarter turned to the left, three-quarter length, hand thrust into waistcoat (characteristic), seated, head supported by right arm, elbow resting on a table. Owner (1922): R. Moorson, 12 Old Burlington St, W. A similar drawing was given by Wordsworth to Annette or Caroline Vallon. A reproduction of the portrait appears in Harper, *Wordsworth, his Life, Works, and Influence*, 1916 and 1929 editions. (*Life and Correspondence of Southey*, ed. C. C. Southey, 1850, vol. v, pp. 50–1; Batho, *Later Wordsworth*, 1933, pp. 331–2. Legouis, *William Wordsworth and Annette Vallon*, p. 109.)

11 *Marble bust by* SIR FRANCIS CHANTREY, 1820.

Executed for Sir George Beaumont. The first mention of any sittings to Chantrey is in Wordsworth's letter to Coleridge of 8 July 1820: "I regret very much having seen so little of you; but this infirmity and my attendance at Chantry's, for my Bust, and numerous other engagements have stood in my way." An incident during the construction of the bust caused Sir Walter Scott to make a tart remark on Wordsworth's vanity. Chantrey's bust of Scott was to accompany that of Wordsworth to an exhibition at the Royal Academy. "I am happy, my effigy is to go with that of W.", wrote Scott to Chantrey's assistant, Allan Cunningham, in 1820, "for (differing from him in many points of taste) I do not know a man more to be venerated for uprightness of heart and loftiness of genius. Why he will sometimes choose to crawl upon all fours

when God has given him so noble a countenance to lift to heaven
I am as little able to account for as for his quarrelling (as you tell
me) with the wrinkles which time and meditation have stamped his
brow withal." When this slight on his character appeared in Lockhart's *Life of Scott* in 1838, Wordsworth wrote Lockhart:

One more word on the story of the Bust. I have a crow to pick
with "honest Allan", he has misled Sir W. by misrepresenting me.
I had not a single wrinkle on my *forehead* at the time when this bust
was executed, and therefore none could be represented by the Artist...
but deep wrinkles I had in my cheeks and the side of my mouth even
from my boyhood—and my wife, who was present while the Bust was
in progress, and remembered them, from the days of her youth, was
naturally wishful to have those peculiarities preserved for the sake of
likeness, in all their force. Chauntrey objected, saying those lines if
given...would sacrifice the spirit to the letter, and by attracting undue
attention, would greatly injure...the resemblances to the living Man.
My own knowledge of art led me to the same conclusion...this is the
plain story, and it is merely told that I may not pass down to posterity
as a Man, whose personal vanity urged him to importune a first-rate
Artist to tell a lie in marble....

In the National Portrait Gallery is Chantrey's preliminary sketch
for the bust, taken with a *camera lucida*, an optical instrument which
makes it possible by means of lenses and prisms to cast the image of
an object on a flat surface so that it can be traced. The bump on the
back of Wordsworth's head is marked by an × on the profile.
Chantrey seems to have traced the head in pencil first, and then to
have corrected it in ink, projecting the nose a bit and bringing in the
chin. Whether the alterations were made in deference to Art or to
the facts it is now impossible to tell.

Whatever its relations to the "living Man", the bust was a huge
success with the poet's friends, relations, and admirers. Wordsworth
immediately ordered seven casts of it at four guineas each, and wanted
to know whether they could be had at a cheaper rate if he ordered
fifteen or twenty. In 1834 the family were still acquiring more casts
of the bust. Sir George was extremely pleased with the bust he had
commissioned, and so extravagant in his praises of it and the artist
that Wordsworth hesitated to repeat them to Chantrey, for fear of
making him blush. People who had never seen Wordsworth considered it "the idea of a poet". In 1845, at the desire of Wordsworth
and Crabb Robinson, an engraving of the bust took the place of an
admittedly poor engraving from the Pickersgill painting (No. 14) in
Moxon's one-volume edition of the poems. The committee formed
to erect a memorial to Wordsworth in 1850 thought first of using the
bust by Chantrey.

But Wordsworth from the first expressed dissatisfaction with the likeness, and though Crabb Robinson liked the bust, he admitted that the head was so generalized that it might be anyone: "It might be Pindar!...or any other individual characterized by profound thought and exquisite sensibility—but I think too that it is a good likeness—and there is a delicacy and grace in the muscles of the cheek which I do not recollect in the Original—I am not pleased with the drapery." Coleridge's comment was guarded: the bust was "more like Wordsworth than Wordsworth was like himself". And Hazlitt, who was always inclined to be hypercritical where Wordsworth was concerned, said bluntly: "It wants marking traits....The bust flatters his head."

Sir Francis Chantrey was an extremely successful sculptor who made busts of two hundred or more of the celebrities of his day. Besides making busts, he made a profitable marriage, and died worth £150,000.

The original bust was at Coleorton Hall, the estate of the Beaumonts near Ashby-de-la-Zouche, in 1889. Crabb Robinson, Wordsworth's wife, his son John, ' two nephews at Cambridge", and a Mr Kenyon are known to have possessed casts of the bust during the poet's lifetime. Edward Moxon owned a bronze cast of it. Chantrey's model for the bust is now in the Ashmolean Museum at Oxford. (*Correspondence of Crabb Robinson with the Wordsworth Circle*, ed. Morley, 1927, pp. 102, 104, 139, 730, 737; *Letters of William and Dorothy Wordsworth: Later Years*, ed. de Selincourt, 1939, pp. 928–9, 707, 1254–5; *Wordsworth's Poetical Works*, ed. Knight, 1889, vol. x, pp. 423–4; Lockhart, *Life of Scott*, 1838, vol. v, p. 40; *D.N.B.* article on Chantrey; *Catalogue of the National Portrait Gallery*, 1950; *Catalogue of Oxford Portraits*, 1912, p. 219.)

12 *Painting by* SIR WILLIAM BOXALL, 1831.

The painting was engraved in 1835 by J. Bromley, and again in 1842 by J. Cochran. It must have been a popular portrait, for in 1847 we still find Wordsworth giving away a print of it. He thought the 1842 engraving beautifully done, though as a likeness he preferred the engraving from Miss Gillies's portrait (No. 20), while admitting that the Boxall "had the advantage, at least, in the outline". In 1832 Boxall did a series of female portraits which were engraved, and he asked Wordsworth to suggest a title for them. The poet's brains, he tells us, were "racked in vain for a title", though he was persuaded that Boxall's paintings would "do him much honour". Edward Quillinan thought him "the *best* painter of abstract female beauty among the artists". Sir William Boxall was a Fellow of the Royal Academy, and became the Director of the National Gallery.

Full-face, half-length. The original belongs to Mrs Dickson at the "Stepping-Stones", Rydal, Ambleside. (*Letters of William and Dorothy Wordsworth: Later Years*, ed. de Selincourt, 1939, pp. 593 and n., 624, 1304; *Wordsworth's Poetical Works*, ed. Knight, 1889, vol. x, p. 410; *D.N.B.* article on Boxall.)

13   Chalk drawing by WILLIAM WILKINS, 1831.

Wilkins transferred this drawing on to stone to make one of the lithographs in his series *Men of the Day*. On 9 September 1831 Dorothy Wordsworth wrote to Catherine Clarkson: "There is just come out a portrait of my Brother, for which he sat when last in London [early 1831]....I think it is a strong likeness, and so does everyone. Of course, to his family something is wanting; nevertheless I value it much as a likeness of him in company, and something of that restraint with cheerfulness, which is natural to him in mixed societies. There is nothing of the poet...." According to Professor Knight, Wordsworth referred to this portrait as "the stamp distributor".

Nearly life-size. There is a photograph of the chalk drawing at "Dove Cottage", Grasmere. The owner (1889) was Mrs Field, Wargreave, nr Henley. (*Wordsworth's Poetical Works*, ed. Knight, 1889, vol. x, pp. 410-11; *Letters of William and Dorothy Wordsworth: Later Years*, ed. de Selincourt, 1939, p. 568; *Catalogue of the Contents of Dove Cottage*, 1947, pp. 13, 33.)

14   Pen-and-ink sketch by DANIEL MACLISE, 1831(?).

Under the name of "Alfred Croquis", Maclise did a series of eighty character portraits of literary men of his time, which were published in *Fraser's Magazine* with a short account of each subject and his work, over the period 1830-8. It is difficult to fix the date of the actual sitting for this portrait. Wordsworth may have sat for it when he was in London in December 1830, or in the spring of 1831 on his way back to Rydal after a stay with his brother Christopher in Sussex. If he did so, it would help to explain a letter of his dated from Rydal, 2 March 1832, in which he referred to "the stupid occupation of sitting to four several artists", when in London "last spring". He must have meant the spring of 1831, and the artists might be Boxall, Wilkins, Maclise, and one not accounted for.

Maclise was a son of a Highlander who became "the greatest historical painter of the English School", to quote the article on him in *D.N.B.* He had a wide acquaintance in literary circles and was a fast friend of Charles Dickens. Of these sketches for *Fraser's Magazine*, some approach good-humoured caricature, some are familiar likenesses, and some are cruel and satiric. The sketch of

Wordsworth falls between the first and second categories. Maclise was famous for his drawing. "His line was somewhat cold and strict, but full of spirit and expression, as elastic and as firm as steel", says *D.N.B.*, and that quality appears to good effect in the sketch of Wordsworth.

Head turned slightly to the right, whole length, seated in a large chair, legs crossed, signature of Wordsworth, and "Author of the Excursion", written underneath. The lithograph from *Fraser's Magazine* in St John's Library is done on a yellow background, but I have seen it on white in a copy of the magazine of the date on which the Wordsworth sketch was printed. (*Letters of William and Dorothy Wordsworth: Later Years*, ed. de Selincourt, 1939, p. 615; *Fraser's Magazine*, October 1832, vol. VI, p. 313.)

15 *Painting by* HENRY WILLIAM PICKERSGILL, 1832.

Executed for St John's College. In the spring of 1831, returning to Rydal after a sojourn in London and Sussex, Wordsworth stayed for a few days at Trinity Lodge, Cambridge. It was on the eve of election, and he was alarmed to find that "the mathematicians of Trinity—Peacock, Airey, Whewell—were taking what I thought the wrong side". He must also at this time have visited his old College, where no doubt he found the political environment more comfortable. At any rate, by 13 June 1831, St John's had become manifestly aware of her poet's existence, and his sister was writing excitedly: "This very moment a letter arrives, very complimentary, from the Master [James Wood] of St John's College, Cambridge (the place of my brother William's education), requesting him to sit for his portrait to some eminent artist, as he expresses it, 'to be placed in the old House among their Worthies'. He writes in his own name and that of several of the Fellows."

Wordsworth's letters at this time show that he, too, felt tremendously honoured and delighted by his College's proposal to paint his portrait. It was a significant testimonial of the rapidly spreading recognition of his greatness as a poet, and de Quincey must have been thinking of it when he wrote in 1835: "Up to 1820 the name of Wordsworth was trampled under foot; from 1820 to 1830 it was militant; from 1830 to 1835 it was triumphant." Wordsworth wrote immediately to the foremost living expert on matters of art, Samuel Rogers, saying:

Let me, my dear friend, have the benefit of your advice upon a small matter of taste. You know that while I was in London I gave more time than a wise man should have done to Portrait-painters and Sculptors [Boxall (No. 12), Wilkins (No. 13), Maclise (No. 14)?, more bust casts from Chantrey (No. 11)?]—I am now called to the same duty again. The Master and a numerous body of the Fellows of my own College, St John's Cambridge, have begged me to sit to some Eminent Artist for my Portrait, to be placed among "the Worthies of that House" of Learning, which has so many claims upon my grateful remembrance.—I consider the application no small honor, and as they have courteously left the choice of the Artist to myself I entreat you would let me have the advantage of your judgment.

Had [John] Jackson [R.A., a very famous portrait painter] been living, without troubling you, I should have enquired of himself whether he would undertake the task; but he is just gone, and I am quite at a loss whom to select. Pray give me your opinion. I saw Pickersgill's pictures at his own house, but between ourselves I did not much like them. [Thomas] Phillips [R.A., painter of Blake, Wilkie, Scott, and Humphry Davy, besides many others] has made Coxcombs of all the Poets, save Crabbe, that have come under his hands, and I am rather afraid he might play that trick with me, grey-headed as I am. [William] Owen [R.A., portrait painter to the Prince of Wales] was a manly painter, but there is the same fault with him as the famous Horse one has heard of—he is departed. In fact, the art is low in England, as you know much better than I—don't, however, accuse me of impertinence, but do as I have desired. . . .

Rogers did so and fixed "on Pickersgill as the best upon the whole".

Pickersgill was a very prolific artist who exhibited 363 pictures at the Academy during his lifetime. According to the *Dictionary of Recent and Living Painters* (1866), "after the death of Phillips he was especially the favourite with those who desired to have large full-length portraits painted for presentation and honorary gifts". Thus the nature of the occasion seems to have determined the artist. It was now only necessary to secure his services and arrange for sittings. Wordsworth called upon his friend Edward Quillinan, who became his son-in-law in 1841, writing him on 4 July 1831:

. . . you know Pickersgill pretty well and perhaps might ascertain for me whether he gives any part of the summer or year to recreation and if so whether he could be tempted to come as far as the Lakes and make my house his headquarters, taking my portrait at the same time; if you do not object to sound him upon such a subject I should thank you to do so, as a reply in the negative might be given with less of a disagreeable feeling through a third person than directly to myself.

He added, being fully aware that Pickersgill must be a very busy man:

I do not think it probable that anything will come of this proposal, but as one of the fellows of the Coll: told me yesterday they wish the thing to be done as soon as may be, I have thought that Mr P. will excuse the liberty I have taken. I ought to add they wish for a half-length, as a size which may range best with the Portraits of the Coll:. . .

The Fellow of St John's with whom Wordsworth corresponded was John Hymers, a tutor, who seems to have been delegated the responsibility of expediting the portrait. In the College Library is a signed letter from the poet to him on that subject; and it was Hymers who collected a subscription of £170 for the portrait, from sixty-nine members of the College.

The plan to entice Pickersgill into the Lake country that summer fell through, and Wordsworth reported the cause to Hymers in a letter of 26 January 1832:

> The proposal to paint my Portrait was made to Mr Pickersgill thro' my friend Mr Quillinan, and an answer received thro' the same channel, which led me to expect Mr P. at Rydal in October last....All that I know is that about the time he was expected here, he was at Paris painting several distinguished Persons there, La Fayette and Cuvier among the number—these engagements probably detained him longer than he expected, as I am at this moment told that it is only a week since he returned to London. I have no doubt but that as soon as Mr Quillinan returns he will see Mr P. and I shall be able to answer more satisfactorily the enquiries which yourself and other Fellows of your Coll: have done me the honour to make upon the subject....

The remainder of the letter has to do with relatives and friends in the University, and it contains the remark: "I congratulate you upon one of your Pupils being so high upon the Tripos—and notice with regret that St John's has not made so great a figure as usual."

Throughout the spring and summer of 1832 the poet and painter were not able to agree on a time and place for the sittings. Pickersgill offered to come to Rydal in May, but Wordsworth had to write that he would be unable to receive him at the time he proposed, being called to Carlisle "on account of public business". As an alternative Wordsworth again suggested to Pickersgill that he combine business with pleasure and visit Rydal during the coming summer. He felt "there was a good deal of delicacy in that proposal, which I was induced to make, not thinking myself justified in putting the College to any further expense than a Portrait from so distinguished an Artist must necessarily impose under ordinary circumstances". Pickersgill invited Wordsworth to come to London and lodge with him while the sittings were in progress. This was impossible because Dorothy Wordsworth was in "so weak and alarming [a] state of health that I could not quit home". In the same letter (5 May) Wordsworth assured the painter that he was under no obligation to come to Rydal to take the portrait, the proposal being made only

> upon a supposition, which proves not to be the fact, that you were in the habit of allotting (as almost all professional men who have leisure, do) a small portion of the Summer to recreation, and I thought the

beauty of the Country...might induce you to come so far....I attach, however, so much interest to the Portrait being from your pencil, that I hope many months may not pass without the College being gratified with a Production which many of its Members are so desirous of possessing.

Wordsworth eventually prevailed and Pickersgill was his guest at Rydal for ten days at the beginning of September 1832. On 12 September Wordsworth wrote to his publisher, Moxon, "Mr Pickersgill is the Bearer of this to London. He has been painting my Portrait—We all like it exceedingly as far as it is carried—it will be finished in London—Should you wish to see it in the present state you can call at his House; but not till a month hence, as it will remain here some little time."

Pickersgill made a sketch for this portrait in red and black chalk, which is considered by several Wordsworthians to be superior to the painting in its delineation of Wordsworth's character. He was sixty-two years old when it was taken, and his biographer Professor Harper writes (1916, vol. II, p. 375), "A close study of the Pickersgill [drawing]...will show that...Wordsworth was already an aged man....Resignation rested like a sunset glow upon his face."

In his letter to Moxon of 12 September 1832 Wordsworth informed him that "in all probability [the painting] will be engraved, but not unless we could secure beforehand 150 Purchasers. I do not say Subscribers for it would [then be] asked as a favour." He wanted Moxon to "receive such names as might offer", but not to advertise in any way. Apparently there were not 150 "such names as might offer", for no such engraving was published at the time. But the poet and his friends do seem to have wished him to appear before the public as Pickersgill had painted him, and in 1836 W. H. Watt engraved the painting for the stereotyped edition of the poems in seven volumes of that year. It continued in the seven subsequent editions, but it was displaced by an engraving after Chantrey (No. 11) in the one-volume edition of 1845. The engraver took a small oval out of the centre of the painting, containing Wordsworth's head and only half his length, and for his pains brought down upon his head the wrath of the Wordsworths. "In following the plan of giving the head and part of the Person, independent of the reclining attitude, an air of feebleness is spread thro' the whole", wrote the poet to Moxon in October 1836. "...We will be much obliged by your having a doz. more prints struck off for us." Still anxious, he wrote again ten days later, "I am still of the opinion, in which others concur, that the attitude has an air of decrepitude in consequence of the whole person not being given." Again, to Henry Taylor in the next month, he complains of the engraving that owing to "its having preserved the inclination of the body...without an arm...to account for it, the whole has an air of feebleness and decrepitude which I hope is not authorized by the subject". In 1845 he stated his opinion of the engraving more strongly to Moxon: "I think I mentioned to you that I had an utter dislike of the Print from Pickersgill prefixed to the Poems. It does me and him also great injustice. Pray what would be the lowest expense of a respectable engraving from Chantrey's Bust?"

It should be noted that Wordsworth blamed the feebleness of the engraving partly on "a fault in the original Picture, of a weakness of expression about the upper lip". He preferred the second likeness taken by Pickersgill in 1840 (No. 22). Even though the poet ordered bad prints of it by the dozen, none of his intimates seems to have been completely satisfied with the St John's portrait. In February 1833, while it was still being finished in London, Wordsworth wrote to Crabb Robinson: "In passing Soho Sq. it may amuse you to call in upon Mr Pickersgill the Portrait Painter where he will...be gratified to introduce you to the face of an old Friend—take Ch. and M. Lamb there also." Crabb Robinson went to Pickersgill's and duly recorded his opinion in his Diary: "It is in every respect a fine picture, except that the artist has made the disease in Wordsworth's eyes too apparent. The picture wants an oculist."

Nevertheless Pickersgill's portrait inspired Wordsworth with a sonnet, as other paintings had done before and would do afterwards. He sent it to the Master and Fellows of St John's. It was published in 1835 with the title *To the Author's Portrait*:

> Go, faithful Portrait! and where long hath knelt
> Margaret, the saintly Foundress, take thy place;
> And, if Time spare the Colors for the grace
> Which to the Work surpassing skill hath dealt,
> Thou, on thy rock reclined, tho' kingdoms melt
> In the hot crucible of Change, wilt seem
> To breathe in rural peace, to hear the Stream,
> To think and feel as once the Poet felt.
> Whate'er thy fate, those features have not grown
> Unrecognized through many a starting tear
> More prompt, more glad to fall, than drops of dew
> By Morning shed around a flower half-blown;
> Tears of delight, that testified how true
> To Life thou art, and, in thy truth, how dear!

Judging from the first line, and from the way the sonnet seems to reflect Wordsworth's first happy reaction to the portrait, it seems probable that he composed it before the portrait went from Rydal to be finished in London, in October of 1832, after it had been part of the family for a month. His concern that time might not "spare the colours" of the painting was a real one, as he demonstrated in his letter to his old classmate Robert Jones, from Trinity Lodge, 1835:

I called upon the Master of St John's [James Wood] yesterday, but did not get to see him, he is said to wear well—I had a friend with me who took me thro' the Lodge and in the Combination room I saw my own Picture...it looks well, but is of too large a size for the room and would be seen to better advantage in the Hall. But had there been room for it there, there is an objection to that place—the charcoal smoke I am told, is ruinous to Pictures, and this which is really well done cost money.

In the Library of St John's College is preserved a relic of this happy visit to Cambridge when Wordsworth first saw his portrait hanging among the "Worthies" of his College. It has never before been published.

Mr Wordsworth, with much pleasure, will do himself the honour of waiting upon the Master & Fellows of St John's to Dinner on Saturday next.

April 1st [1835]
Trin. Lodge   The Master of St John's C.C.
                                                         St John's Coll.

The words of the conventional social formula must here have expressed the writer's true feelings. The sight of his portrait hanging in his college must have been a sign of victory to the boy who once refused to take the advice of his guardians and tutors, but who lived to make their descendants recognize his real powers on his own terms, and such recognition goes far to explain the overtones of self-esteem which occur in Wordsworth's letters about the portrait.

See plate of painting facing p. 129, and plate of drawing facing p. 128. The drawing now hangs in the Combination Room of the College, and the painting is in the Hall. (*Letters of William and Dorothy Wordsworth: Later Years*, ed. de Selincourt, 1939, pp. 556–7, 558, 559–60, 598–9 (MS. at St John's), 619–20 (MS. at St John's), 620–1 (MS. at St John's), 630–1, 734, 806–7, 808–9, 814–5, 1041, 1254–5; Harper, *Life of Wordsworth*, 1916, vol. II, p. 375; Oxford *Wordsworth*, 1939, p. xxx; *Crabb Robinson's Diary*, ed. Sadler, 1869, vol. III, p. 25; I have given the version of the sonnet from the MS. at St John's; the invitation acceptance and the list of subscribers to the portrait are unpublished MSS. at St John's.)

16 *Painting by* HENRY HALL PICKERSGILL (son of H. W.), 1835.

Executed for Dora, Wordsworth's daughter. This portrait is a smaller version of the senior Pickersgill's portrait for St John's

College, but based partly on new sittings. Crabb Robinson notes in his diary for 3 March 1835: "I walked with the Wordsworth's to Pickersgill, who is painting a small likeness of the poet for Dora. We sat there for a couple of hours, enlivening by chat the dulness of sitting for a portrait", and later on 14 March: "I called on Wordsworth, by appointment, at Pickersgill's. The small picture of Wordsworth is much better than the large one." The family, as usual, were difficult to please: "Mary says it has a lackadaisical look."

Similar to No. 15, facing p. 129. The junior Pickersgill made a copy of it for Christopher Wordsworth, Master of Trinity. Owner (1923) Miss E. Kennedy of Capri; another similar portrait was presented as heirloom to Brinsop Court, Hereford, by Lord Saye and Sele. (*Crabb Robinson's Diary*, ed. Sadler, 1869, vol. III, pp. 61, 62; *Letters of William and Dorothy Wordsworth: Later Years*, ed. de Selincourt, 1939, p. 1041.)

17 *Wax medallion by* WILLIAM WYON, 1835.

Robert Southey gives us the circumstances of its creation in a letter of 29 September 1835:

Mr Wyon has killed two birds with one shot. Seeing how perfectly satisfied everybody here was with his medallion of me, he asked for an introduction to W., which I was about to have offered him. Off he set in good spirits to Rydal, and not finding W. there, was advised to follow him to Lowther. To Lowther he went, and came back from thence delighted with his own success, and with the civilities of Lord and Lady Lonsdale, who desired that they might have both medallions. Nothing, I think, can be better than W.'s, and he is equally pleased with mine.

Wordsworth communicated his equal pleasure to Southey from Lowther Castle:

I am glad you liked the Medallion; I was anxious for your opinion of it, and more particularly as it was not to be seen by my Friends and Family at Rydal. Mr. Wyon seemed a person of agreeable and gentlemanly manners: In common with all here, I thought his likeness of you a very successful one, and I shall be very glad to *hang* in such good company.

Wyon was chief engraver to the Mint, a fine medallist, and famed for his skill in portrait-taking.

Head, profile to the left, 3¼ in. diameter. Now in the National Portrait Gallery. In a letter of 19 February 1840 Wordsworth mentions *two medallions* which have been sent to Wyon to be "improved". (*Letters of William and Dorothy Wordsworth: Later Years*, ed. de Selincourt, 1939, pp. 757 and n., 1004; *Catalogue of the National Portrait Gallery*, 1949.)

18 *Painting by* JOSEPH SEVERN, 1837.

In 1837 Wordsworth went on a six-month tour through France and Italy to Rome, with Crabb Robinson. Reporting to his family from Albano in May, he wrote:

Of persons we have seen not many, and these chiefly English Artists who by the by seem to live at Rome on very good terms with each other. One of them Mr Severn, the Friend of Keats the Poet, has taken my portrait which I mean to present to Isabella [the wife of his son John]. I fear you will not, nor will she, be satisfied with it, it is thought however to be a likeness as to features, only following the fact, he has made me look at least four years older than I did when I walked 7 hours in Paris without resting and without fatigue.

As soon as he got back to London he wrote to Rydal, having sent the painting on ahead: "Don't send the portrait to Isabella till I come. I will get it framed if she thinks it worth it, which I fear she will not, nor you either." Isabella did accept it, however, because the portrait stayed in the family, eventually descending to grandson William Wordsworth, Principal of Elphinstone College, Bombay. In 1882 he wrote a description of it to Professor Knight: "I neither consider it a pleasing picture, nor a satisfactory likeness. . . He is represented. . . with the air and attitude. . . of an elderly citizen, waiting for a 'bus. . . . I think I have heard that Wordsworth himself said that it made him look more like a banker than a poet; perhaps he ought to have said a stamp-distributor." In Severn's defence it may be said that by the time Wordsworth was sixty-seven, with a shrewd eye for the price of busts, prints, and canal shares, he may well have looked as much like a banker as a poet.

Full length, seated, with an umbrella in his hand. In 1923 it was in the possession of Miss E. Kennedy of Capri. (*Letters of William and Dorothy Wordsworth: Later Years*, ed. de Selincourt, 1939, pp. 858–9, 895; *Wordsworth's Poetical Works*, ed. Knight, 1889, vol. x, pp. 411–12.)

19 *Miniature painting on ivory by* MARGARET GILLIES, 1839.

This painting was commissioned by Moon for the purpose of engraving. In a letter to Professor Knight in 1882, Miss Gillies misdated her series of portraits of Wordsworth and his family, giving it as 1841, thus laying a trap into which a considerable number of Wordsworthians have fallen. F. V. Morley's *Dora Wordsworth, her Book*, and Professor de Selincourt's edition of the *Letters* prove that all of Miss Gillies's portraits were taken in the year 1839. The poet's daughter is the first member of the family to mention Miss Gillies's portrait-taking visit to Rydal in *Her Book* for early 1839.

Wordsworth's letters, however, took no notice of her presence until
1 November 1839, when he wrote to the publisher Moxon: "Miss
Gillies an artist who paints in miniature of whom you may have
heard has come down from London on purpose to take my portrait
and it is thought she has succeeded admirably. She will carry the
picture to London...." The picture was duly engraved by Edward
MacInnes and published by Moon on 6 August 1841. Miss Gillies
thought it "was not a very good representation of the picture".
The portrait inspired one of Wordsworth's friends with a sonnet,
of which I will include a fragment as an interesting specimen of
nineteenth-century Wordsworthianism.

> Here I seem to gaze
> On Wordsworth's honoured face; for in the cells
> Of those deep eyes Thought like a prophet dwells,
> And round those drooping lips Song like a murmur strays.
>
> (THOMAS POWELL)

These lines catch the spirit of the portrait perfectly.

Miss Margaret Gillies was an orphan at an early age, who boldly
resolved to support herself as a professional painter. She taught
herself the art and made a success as a miniaturist.

Three-quarter face turned to the left, full length, seated at a table. In
1889 the original was in the possession of Sir Henry Doulton, Lambeth.
(*Letters of William and Dorothy Wordsworth: Later Years*, ed. de Selincourt,
1939, p. 987; *Wordsworth's Poetical Works*, ed. Knight, 1889, vol. x, pp. 415–
17; S. V. Morley, *Dora Wordsworth, her Book*, 1924, p. 160; *D.N.B.* article
on Miss Gillies.)

20 *Miniature painting on ivory by* MARGARET GILLIES, 1839.

A painting of the poet and his wife, ordered by them.
"The second portrait was similar in position to the first", wrote
Miss Gillies, "the Wordsworths being so pleased with the one done
for Moon, as to wish it repeated for themselves, with the addition
of Mrs Wordsworth at the poet's side." The following passage from
a fragment of a letter of Wordsworth's to Thomas Powell must refer
to one of the copies of this portrait that Miss Gillies made for the
family: "...when you see Miss Gillies pray tell her that she is remembered in this house with much pleasure and great affection....Her
picture has just arrived, and appears to be much approved; but of
course as to the degree of likeness in each [subject] there is a great
diversity of opinion...." The fragmentary MS. of this letter,
probably written early in 1840, is in St John's College Library.

Wordsworth sits at the right-hand of a table, exactly as he did in No. 19,
but this painting has been made twice as wide as No. 19, so as to include the
other half of the table and Mrs Wordsworth seated there, turned to the

right, appearing in her role of amanuensis. The original descended to grandson William Wordsworth in Bombay, where it was accidentally burnt. But Miss Gillies had made two copies. One of these was made for Dora (Wordsworth) Quillinan, and it or the other is now to be seen at "Dove Cottage", Grasmere. (*Wordsworth's Poetical Works*, ed. Knight, 1889, vol. X, pp. 416–17; *Letters of William and Dorothy Wordsworth: Later Years*, ed. de Selincourt, 1939, p. 1001 (MS. at St John's); *Catalogue of Dove Cottage*, 1947.)

21 *Miniature painting on ivory by* MARGARET GILLIES, 1839.

"I think you will be delighted, with a Profile picture on ivory of me, with which Miss G. is at this moment engaged [late 1839], Mrs. W. seems to prefer it as a likeness to anything she has yet done...." It was indeed a popular picture for it was often reproduced in nineteenth-century editions of the works. It has been given prominence more recently in Miss Morley's *Correspondence of Crabb Robinson with the Wordsworth Circle*.

Profile turned to the left, half-length, right elbow on table and right hand resting on right shoulder, wearing his cloak. In 1927 the original was owned by Mr Gordon Wordsworth, "Stepping Stones", Ambleside. (*Letters of William and Dorothy Wordsworth: Later Years*, ed. de Selincourt, 1939, pp. 993–4; *Wordsworth's Poetical Works*, ed. Knight, 1889, vol. X, pp. 416–17.)

22 *Painting by* HENRY WILLIAM PICKERSGILL, 1840.

Done for Sir Robert Peel's Gallery of Living Authors at Drayton Manor. The earliest mention of this portrait is in Wordsworth's letter to Pickersgill of 29 June 1840, the manuscript of which now belongs to St John's College. Pickersgill had proposed that he come to Rydal to paint the picture and most of the letter concerns Wordsworth's efforts to find lodgings for him, his own house being full of guests until September. Another letter in St John's Library of 3 September [1840] postpones for a fortnight an engagement with Pickersgill because it conflicts with a previously planned trip to Lord Lonsdale's with Samuel Rogers. By 17 September Pickersgill had come and gone. Recalling the occasion a year later, Wordsworth wrote: "It was generally thought here that this work was more successful as the likeness than the one painted some years ago for St John's College." It was still not good enough for Coleridge's daughter Sara, however, who vehemently declared her opinion after the poet's death:

Pickersgill's portrait of our dear departed great poet is *insufferable*— velvet waistcoat, neat shiny boots,—just the sort of dress he would not have worn if you could have hired him—and a sombre sentimentalism of countenance quite unlike his own look, which was either elevated with high gladness or deep thought, or at times simply and childishly gruff; but never tender after that fashion, so lackadaisical and mawkishly sentimental.

Sara may have been thinking of the junior Pickersgill's portrait (No. 16), but the "velvet waistcoat" and "neat shiny boots" are certainly not attributes of the St John's portrait (No. 15).

See reproduction facing p. 120. The pose is almost identical with that of No. 15, but it includes the legs, and Wordsworth is not wearing his cape. Some flowers have been added in the foreground. The original may be seen at the Wordsworth Museum, Grasmere; there is a replica of the portrait, by Pickersgill, in the National Portrait Gallery. (*Letters of William and Dorothy Wordsworth: Later Years*, ed. de Selincourt, 1939, pp. 1028 (MS. at St John's), 1034 (MS. at St John's); *Wordsworth and Reed*, ed. Broughton, 1933, p. 42; *Catalogue of the National Portrait Gallery*, 1949; *Catalogue of Dove Cottage*, 1947, p. 30; Beatty, *William Wordsworth of Rydal Mount*, 1939, p. 135.)

23 *Painting of Wordsworth on Helvellyn by* BENJAMIN HAYDON, 1842.

In 1839 Haydon finished his portrait of Wellington musing on the battlefield of Waterloo twenty years after his victory. It had been a labour of love. In August 1840 he sent a print of it to Wordsworth. The noble prospect inspired a sonnet, beginning

> By Art's bold privilege, Warrior and War-horse stand
> On ground yet strewn with their last battle's wreck.

"It was actually composed", wrote Wordsworth to Haydon on 4 September, "while I was climbing Helvellyn last Monday. My daughter and Mr Quillinan were with me; and she, which I believe had scarcely ever been done before, rode every inch of the way to the summit, and a magnificent day we had." The sonnet in turn inspired a painting, of the poet in the act of composing it. We learn from the poet's letter of 13 January 1841 that Haydon wished to paint

not a mere matter-of-fact portrait, but one of a poetical character... in some favourite scene of these mountains. I am rather afraid, I own, of any attempt of this kind; but, if he keeps in his present mind, which I doubt, it would be vain to oppose his inclination. He is a great enthusiast, possessed also of a most active intellect; but he wants that submissive and steady good sense, which is absolutely necessary for the adequate development of power, in that art to which he is attached.

But Haydon persevered in his intention, and on 12 June 1842 wrote in his journal: "Saw dear Wordsworth, who promised to sit at three.

Wordsworth sat and looked venerable, but I was tired with the heat....I made a successful sketch. He comes again tomorrow."

Wordsworth was delighted with the painting when it was finished, and said: "I myself think it is the best likeness, that is, the most characteristic, that has been done of me." It was his considered opinion, given four years after the painting of the portrait. He expressed some reservations, however, in a letter to his American editor, Reed, during the same year: "There is great merit in this work and the sight of it will shew my meaning on the subject of *expression*. This I think is attained, but then, I am stooping and the inclination of the head necessarily causes a foreshortening of the features below the nose which takes from the likeness accordingly...."

One more sonnet completes the cycle started by the painting of Wellington on his horse "Copenhagen". At the request of their mutual friend, Miss Mitford, Haydon sent his portrait of Wordsworth to Elizabeth Barrett, who produced the following lines forthwith:

> Wordsworth upon Helvellyn! Let the cloud
> Ebb audibly along the mountain wind,
> Then break against the rock, and show behind
> The lowland valleys floating up to crowd
> The sense with beauty. *He*, with forehead bowed,
> And humble-lidded eyes, as one inclined
> Before the sovran thoughts of his own mind,
> And very meek with inspirations proud,
> Takes here his rightful place, as Poet-Priest
> By the high Altar, singing praise and prayer
> To the higher Heavens. A noble vision free
> Our Haydon's hand hath flung from out the mist!
> No Portrait this with Academic air,
> *This* is the Poet and his Poetry.

Miss Barrett sent a copy of her sonnet to Wordsworth, who wrote from Rydal on 26 October 1842: "The conception of your sonnet is in full accordance with the Painter's intended work, and the expression vigorous; yet the word 'ebb' though I do not myself object to it...will I fear prove obscure to nine readers out of ten...." A member of the rising generation was now initiated into the mysteries of the curious interlocking of literature and painting that was so characteristic of her century. She had written a sonnet composed upon a painting of a poet composing a sonnet on a painting.

Four days before he wrote "Finis of B. R. Haydon" in his journal, Haydon made the entry: "I sent the Duke, Wordsworth, dear Fred's and Mary's heads, to Miss Barrett to protect." If the world was soon to crash in pieces around him, at least these beloved paintings would be in safe hands.

At some time during the years 1842–6 Haydon conceived of painting Wordsworth *seated* on Helvellyn, for a correspondent of Professor Knight's possessed in 1889 an unfinished painting of that description. The head was done in great detail and the painting included a view of the lake flashing beneath the mountain, and an "eagle perched on a crag" overhead. Knight's correspondent believed that it was painted when Wordsworth was last in London before Haydon's death, which would mean it was painted in May 1845. Haydon made no mention of even seeing Wordsworth on this visit to London. I suspect that he started the painting in 1843, working from his various sketches, his life mask, and his memory. This hypothesis is substantiated by Wordsworth's letter to the artist which Professor de Selincourt dates "[July 1843?]" in which the poet fears much "that the Picture you are doing of me upon Helvellyn, as it is not done by commission, may disappoint you." Since Miss Barrett had already written her sonnet on the standing portrait sent to her the year before, Wordsworth must have been referring to the seated portrait, and his advice may account for its having been left unfinished.

Miss Barrett's sonnet was printed for the first time in *The Eagle* of 1877; the lateness of publication may be attributed to the scorn she expressed at portraits "with Academic air", which may have seemed to be directed at the works of Pickersgill. In 1891, at the urging of the then Dr J. E. Sandys, the historian of classical scholarship, and a Fellow of St John's, the College considered buying Haydon's last finished picture of Wordsworth for 250 guineas from a Miss Nicholson, whose father had bought it at the sale of Haydon's effects in 1852, and whose two nephews had been Fellows of the College. In spite of Dr Sandys's emphasis in his letters to the Master on everything that might possibly be said for the Haydon portrait, and against the Pickersgill portrait which hung in the Hall, the College did not acquire it, and it went to an individual buyer, eventually finding a place in the National Portrait Gallery in 1920.

Miss Nicholson, through Dr Sandys, gave the College in 1895 "a handsomely framed permanent photograph" of her portrait of Wordsworth. The gift is described in *The Eagle* for 1895, which records some writing on the back of the original which I have seen nowhere else: "The artist wrote the date (1842) with a quotation from Wordsworth:—'High is our calling, friend.'" Although the National Portrait Gallery has made no record of any such writing, it may well have been there at one time, for towards the end of his tortured existence Haydon wrote to Wordsworth that one of the four greatest days in his life was the day he received the sonnet beginning with those lines.

See reproduction facing p. 120. Three-quarter length, standing, three-quarters turned to the left, head bowed, arms folded, Helvellyn and clouds in the background. The portrait from the National Portrait Gallery is reproduced in colour in D. Wellesley, *English Poets in Pictures: Wordsworth*, 1942. The unfinished portrait of Wordsworth is at "Dove Cottage", Grasmere. Haydon's "successful sketch" for the portrait has vanished. (*Life of Haydon*, ed. Tom Taylor, 1853, vol. III, pp. 131, 138, 160–2, 223, 237, 327, 349; *Wordsworth and Reed*, ed. Broughton, 1933, pp. 42, 160; *Catalogue of the National Portrait Gallery*, 1949, which includes a plate; correspondence in St John's Library of C. M. Stuart, J. E. Sandys, and J. R. Tanner with the Master of the College, 1891; *Wordsworth's Poetical Works*, ed. Knight, 1889, vol. X, pp. 417–19; *Letters of William and Dorothy Wordsworth: Later Years*, ed. de Selincourt, 1939, pp. 1144, 1172; *Eagle*, 1895, vol. XVIII, p. 212; I have printed the version of Miss Barrett's sonnet given in *The Eagle*, 1877, vol. X, p. 151.)

24 *Bust by* ANGUS FLETCHER, *between* 1842 *and* 1844.

Fletcher's mother was a summer resident at Lancrigg near Grasmere and a great friend of the Wordsworths. His niece wrote to Professor Knight in 1889 that "the Wordsworth head is very like in air and expression, and much more like than the medallion in the Church [at Grasmere, by Woolner]." Angus Fletcher studied under Chantrey and did busts of Mrs Hemans and Joanna Baillie.

In 1889 the bust was at Lancrigg. (*Wordsworth's Poetical Works*, ed. Knight, 1889, vol. X, pp. 424–5; Beatty, *William Wordsworth of Rydal Mount*, 1939, pp. 10, 13, 145.)

25 *Painting by* HENRY INMAN, 1844.

Executed for Professor Henry Reed, Wordsworth's American editor. The first news of this portrait is contained in Reed's letter to Wordsworth, 28 June 1844: "Mr Inman, who for several years has stood at the head of his profession in this country as a portrait painter, has lately sailed for Europe." Would Wordsworth sit to him for a portrait? He would, and he wrote Crabb Robinson in July, asking him to look out for the painter in London. Inman came to Rydal in August 1844 and swept the Wordsworths off their feet: "Have you been told of the New Portrait? the last & best that has been taken of the Poet—", wrote Mary Wordsworth on 23 September, "The painter is an American—deputed to carry the Laureate's Head to our unseen friend Mr Reed of Philadelphia. And thither ere this the picture is on its way....[It] appears to us a marvel inasmuch as it only occupied the Artist & Sitter scarcely 4½ hours to produce it. All agreed that no Englishman could do the like." Inman was as happy about his visit as the Wordsworths, and reported to Reed in America that Wordsworth "evidently had a peculiar value for this transatlantic compliment to his genius....

When the picture was finished, he said all that should satisfy my anxious desire for a successful termination to my labours. His wife, son, and daughter all expressed their approval of my work. He told me he had sat twenty-seven times to various artists, and that my picture was the best likeness of them all." Later the poet was not so sure that the expression of the face in the portrait came up to his highest expectations, but he admitted that it met perfectly the artist's intention.

After returning to New York, Inman painted a replica of the original, which he and Professor Reed presented to the Wordsworths as a Christmas gift. While at Rydal, Inman had made sketches of the grounds which he converted into an oil painting in America. He introduced a representation of himself painting the view, and Wordsworth watching him, on the middle ground of the landscape, but died before he completed the painting. Wordsworth's head is unfortunately half-hidden by a large hat.

The portrait is a three-quarter face turned to the right, quarter-length. Both the original and the unfinished landscape are now in the Library of the University of Pennsylvania, and the replica is owned by the Rev. Christopher W. Wordsworth, of Dedham Oak, Dedham, Essex. Professor Broughton reproduced both the landscape and the original portrait in *Wordsworth and Reed*, 1933, and Miss Beatty used the replica as frontispiece to her *William Wordsworth of Rydal Mount*, 1939. (*Wordsworth and Reed*, ed. Broughton, 1933, pp. 124, 155, 156, 157, 160, 163; *Correspondence of Crabb Robinson with the Wordsworth Circle*, ed. Morley, 1927, pp. 567, 571; *Wordsworth's Poetical Works*, ed. Knight, 1889, vol. x, pp. 420–2.)

26 *Sketch of Wordsworth and Hartley Coleridge at Rydal by* JOHN PETER MULCASTER, 1844.

In a recent letter to the Editor, Mr Cecil Mumford of "Tylehurst Close", Forest Row, Sussex, describes a water-colour taken from this sketch, now in his possession. On the water-colour is written: "After a sketch from the life made in 1844 by John Peter Mulcaster." It "shows the *back* view of the two, walking by the shore of the lake, Wordsworth in wide-brimmed hat & brown frock coat, & H. C. a ridiculous little figure in top hat of beaver & a black or dark-blue coat".

27 *Sketch from memory by* JANE PASLEY, 1845.

Inman's portrait was the last official painting of Wordsworth before his death, but during the remaining six years of his life he seems to have sat to a number of Lakeland painters and sketchers. He had already become an established part of the scenery. The original of the Pasley sketch and an etching plate from it by John Bull are now at "Dove Cottage", Grasmere. Across the street in the Wordsworth Museum is an etching from the plate. I saw the sketch some time ago and remember it as a very interesting piece of work. I have been unable to discover Miss Pasley's name in any of the usual sources of information about artists.

Catalogue of Dove Cottage, 1947, pp. 23, 33.

28   *Sketch by an artist, living in* 1889, 1845.

In Professor Knight's list of the portraits in volume ten of the *Poetical Works* is this statement: "I have also heard of a sketch of the poet, taken in Rydal Church, in the year 1845, by a living artist, an eminent portrait painter; but as it has been lost for the present, description of it in detail is unnecessary" (p. 431).

29   *Portrait by* MISS MACINNES, 1846.

The Catalogue of Dove Cottage lists an "Engraving by Edward MacInnes of a portrait by Miss MacInnes. 1846" (p. 33). It is a full-face portrait, half-length, with the poet's right elbow on the arm of a divan, his right hand supporting his head.

30   *Medal by* LEONARD WYON, 1847.

In April of 1847, Wordsworth sat for a medal to Leonard Wyon, whose father William had already made a medallion of the poet (No. 17). Young Wyon, a friend of Crabb Robinson, was an engraver like his father, and he seems to have come all the way to Rydal to make a medal of the poet in order to increase his reputation in the profession. On 2 April 1847, Wordsworth mentions sittings to Wyon in a note to Crabb Robinson: "At 10 on Monday morning your Medalist friend comes again to me, so that, if it should suit you to call at that time, you would be sure to find me at home...." On 2 May he was still sitting for the medal, as Robinson's letter of that date proves: "Monday—I attended Wordsworth while he sat to have his face modelled by the Son of Wyon the dye-sinker. Probably a medal too will be struck." In January of 1848 the elder Wyon wrote to thank Robinson for introducing his son "to the great Man", and to announce that the medal was finished and awaiting his approval. Wyon added: "I may be permitted to express the pleasure it has afforded to me to find that he has preserved the likeness of the Poet & the execution is such that I think it will do him no discredit at any future time...." When the "future time" came, his son Leonard was appointed chief engraver to the Mint.

The sittings in April 1847 also produced a chalk drawing, which Professor Knight has pronounced to be "the best—perhaps the most characteristic of all the portraits".

Both the drawing and the medal are heads in profile. In the drawing the head is turned to the right, and under it is written: ' William Wordsworth/ April 21st 1847/aetat—77—." Drawing now owned by Mrs Dickson, "Stepping-Stones", Rydal, Ambleside; the Wordsworth Museum, Grasmere, has a photograph of it, and an impression of the medal on silver. (*Correspondence of Crabb Robinson with the Wordsworth Circle*, ed. Morley, 1927, pp. 633, 645, 646; Knight, *English Lake District*, 1891, p. xv, frontispiece a reproduction of the drawing; *Catalogue of Dove Cottage*, 1947, pp. 19, 33.)

31 *Miniature in water-colour by* THOMAS CARRICK, 1847.

The only reference to the painter in the published correspondence of Wordsworth is to "Mr Carrick, a miniature painter, who took my portrait when I met him not long ago at his native place, Carlisle". The letter is dated 16 March 1848. Carrick was a famous miniaturist who exhibited frequently at the Royal Academy, from 1841 to 1866. His portrait of Carlyle is one of his most notable performances.

Mr G. Wordsworth, of "Stepping-Stones", Rydal, Ambleside, owned the original. Knight heard that Carrick made a copy for " the late Lord Bradford". (*Letters of William and Dorothy Wordsworth: Later Years*, ed. de Selincourt, 1939, p. 131 and n.; *Wordsworth's Poetical Works*, ed. Knight, 1889, vol. x, p. 423.)

32 *Two charcoal sketches by* SAMUEL LAWRENCE, *date unknown*.

These sketches were taken in the poet's old age. J. Dykes Campbell, who owned them in 1889, told Professor Knight that "Lawrence was perhaps the most faithful reproducer of men's features of his day". Judging from the dates of Lawrence's paintings, given in *D.N.B.*, his greatest activity as a painter began after 1840. He was a member of the Society of British Artists.

Head only. One original sketch and a photograph, probably of the other, may be seen at "Dove Cottage", Grasmere. (*Wordsworth's Poetical Works*, ed. Knight, 1889, vol. x, p. 429; *D.N.B.*, who spell his name " Laurence"; *Catalogue of Dove Cottage*, 1947, p. 14.)

33 *Drawing on wood by* JACOB THOMPSON, *date unknown*.

In his biography of the artist, Llewellyn Jewitt writes:

Jacob Thompson designed two illustrative pictures which he himself drew on the wood, and presented ready for engraving to his friend Mr S. C. Hall, for his *Social Notes*. The first of these, commemorative of Wordsworth, bears in the circle an original portrait of the Laureate, and a composition landscape which includes...Rydal Mount, Rydal Water...the mountains, and, in the foreground...one of the poet's own creations, the simple pastoral of Barbara Lewthwaite and her pet Lamb.

Hall's *Social Notes* were published weekly, from 1878 to 1881. Thompson was a friend of Wordsworth, described in *Bryan's Dictionary of Painters and Engravers*, 1905, as "a clever landscape painter". The portrait represents Wordsworth in advanced middle life.

Head and bust, three-quarter face turned to the left. The engraving appears in the *Life and Works of Thompson*, by L. Jewitt, 1882. It might be anybody. (Jewitt, *Thompson*, pp. 102–6; *Wordsworth's Poetical Works*, ed. Knight, 1889, vol. x, pp. 427–8.)

34? *Portrait in the London* Times, *22 April* 1950, *date unknown.*

The caption reads: "An oil painting of Wordsworth, found in a Lakeland garage....It carries no clue to the artist's identity, but is thought to have been painted between 1843 and 1850." Mr Maurice Dodd, who is custodian of Wordsworth House, Cockermouth, and who found the portrait, has been kind enough to write to me at length concerning it. He tells me that it was the consensus of opinion of those who visited the poet's birthplace during the centenary celebrations of this year that the subject of the portrait is Wordsworth. In his opinion the likeness was probably taken about the year 1815 by a roving portrait painter of the sort common in the Lake District during the early nineteenth century. I think that the picture may have been painted even earlier, because it shows a pretty good head of hair for Wordsworth in 1815, when he already was speaking of baldness at the crown (No. 6). One immediately thinks of the lost portrait by Hazlitt (No. 3) which Coleridge considered "20 years too old" for Wordsworth, as a happy solution to the problem of identification. Mr J. W. Nicholas of Cockermouth has very kindly sent me a good photograph of Mr Dodd's discovery which shows that the painting is very crudely executed and is not to be compared with the finished work Hazlitt displays in his portrait of Lamb, done in 1804. Though the known facts about Hazlitt's portrait do not exclude the new find, there must be more positive evidence before the Hazlitt hypothesis can be proved.

See reproduction facing p. 120.

One of the portraits in Professor Knight's list in vol. x of the *Poetical Works* never existed at all. He based his knowledge of it on his own reading of Wordsworth's scrawled letter to Crabb Robinson of 24 June 1817: "I have not lately...seen any one new thing whatever, except a bust of myself. Some kind person—which persons mostly unknown to me are—has been good enough to forward me this." Miss Morley, who uncovered Knight's error in her *Correspondence of Crabb Robinson with the Wordsworth Circle* (pp. viii–ix), was able to decipher the passage correctly as: "I have not seen... any one new thing whatever except abuse of myself and sometimes praise, which persons mostly unknown to me are officious enough to forward." This makes much better sense.

* * * * *

This article includes only those portraits which were taken from life, but I should perhaps draw attention to two of Wordsworth's most public portraits—the fine medallion by Thomas Woolner in Grasmere Church, and Frederick Thrupp's statue in the Baptistry of Westminster Abbey. They were both done after the poet's death. Woolner based his medallion on paintings and the bust by Angus Fletcher (No. 24), and Thrupp made use of the Haydon life mask (No. 5).

I am much indebted to Professor Knight's appendix, "The Portraits of Wordsworth", for important facts about many of the likenesses. As the chief Wordsworthian of his age he had seen or heard about most of them. But neither he nor I have been able to crowd in twenty-six portraits before the Inman painting of 1844 (No. 25), in order to fit Wordsworth's statement that he had "sat twenty-seven times to various artists" at that time. Even though my total of twenty-five includes one portrait that was unknown to Knight, he was able to arrive at twenty-six by counting his invented bust and including a replica or a copy, disregarding the fact that the poet based his calculation on sittings only. The chronological disorder of Knight's list makes it difficult to tell just how he did arrive at that figure. There were forty-four portraits in Knight's whole list, but he did not include No. 4, the sketches for Nos. 11 and 15, or Nos. 26, 27, 29, 30 and 34. If we suppose that Wordsworth was both vain and matter-of-fact enough in his old age to have counted accurately the number of times he sat for his portrait, we must assume that two portraits before Inman's are missing from this catalogue: one might easily be No. 26, by Mulcaster. But if we consider both the informal character of many of the likenesses taken after 1844, and the very minor reputation of the artists who descended on Rydal to get a picture of the great poet during those six final years, it is evident that more than one or two portraits may still be in existence which are not in this catalogue. B. R. S.

PORTRAIT OF WORDSWORTH IN PENCIL AND CHALK
BY R. HANCOCK
No. 2

ST JOHN'S COLLEGE FROM FISHER'S LANE BEFORE 1814

FIRST COURT, F2, OCCUPIED BY WORDSWORTH, 1787–91

PORTRAIT OF WORDSWORTH
IN PENCIL AND CHALK
BY B. R. HAYDON

No. 9

PORTRAIT OF WORDSWORTH(?)
BY UNKNOWN ARTIST

No. 34

PORTRAIT FROM
"WORDSWORTH ON HELVELLYN"
BY B. R. HAYDON

No. 23

PORTRAIT OF WORDSWORTH BY
H. W. PICKERSGILL IN
NATIONAL PORTRAIT GALLERY

No. 22

PORTRAIT OF WORDSWORTH BY H. W. PICKERSGILL IN
ST JOHN'S COLLEGE HALL

No. 15

To my Portrait
Painted by Pickersgill at Rydal Mount
For St. John's College Cambridge

Go, faithful Portrait! & where long hath knelt
Margaret, the saintly Foundress, take thy place;
And if Time spare the Colors for the grace
Which to the work surpassing shall hath dealt
Thou, on thy rock reclined, the kingdoms melt
In the hot crucible of Change, wilt seem
To breathe in rural peace, to hear the stream,
To think and feel as once the Poet felt.
Whate'er thy fate, those features have not grown
Unrecognized thro' many a starting tear
More prompt, more glad to fall, than drops of dew
Thy morning shed around a flower half-blown;
Tears of delight that testified how true
To Life thou art, and, in thy truth, how dear!

Wm Wordsworth

FACSIMILE OF SONNET ON PORTRAIT

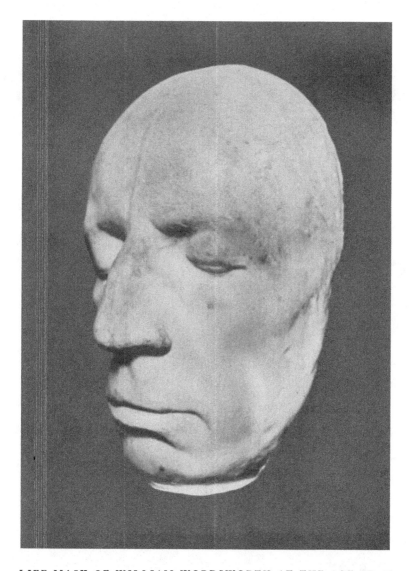

LIFE MASK OF WILLIAM WORDSWORTH AT THE AGE OF 45

A photograph taken by W. F. Dunn, of the cast given to
St John's College by Mrs Butler in 1918.
Now in the College Library.

No. 5

Printed in the United States
By Bookmasters